CW00825556

See page 194.

The Glory Of The Sea, By Darley Dale

Francesca Maria Steele

Nabu Public Domain Reprints:

You are holding a reproduction of an original work published before 1923 that is in the public domain in the United States of America, and possibly other countries. You may freely copy and distribute this work as no entity (individual or corporate) has a copyright on the body of the work. This book may contain prior copyright references, and library stamps (as most of these works were scanned from library copies). These have been scanned and retained as part of the historical artifact.

This book may have occasional imperfections such as missing or blurred pages, poor pictures, errant marks, etc. that were either part of the original artifact, or were introduced by the scanning process. We believe this work is culturally important, and despite the imperfections, have elected to bring it back into print as part of our continuing commitment to the preservation of printed works worldwide. We appreciate your understanding of the imperfections in the preservation process, and hope you enjoy this valuable book.

THE GLORY OF THE SEA

BY

DARLEY DALE

AUTHOR OF 'THE GREAT AUK'S EGG,' 'SWALLOWTAILS AND SKIPPERS,' ETC.

WITH ILLUSTRATIONS BY CHARLES WHYMPER

AND

A TABLE OF THE PRINCIPAL BRITISH SHELLS.

LONDON :

THE RELIGIOUS TRACT SOCIETY,

56, PATERNOSTER ROW ; 65, ST. PAUL'S CHURCHYARD :

AND 164, PICCADILLY.

Richard Clay and Sons,

London and Bungay.

CONTENTS.

LIST OF ILLUSTRATIONS.

THE GLORY OF THE SEA.

CHAPTER I.

MISS CRABBE'S WILL.

'The sea is His, and He made it.'—PSALM xcv. 5.

'AN eccentric will, sir; a very eccentric will,' said the lawyer, as he folded up the document in question, and returned it to its home in a tin case labelled 'Miss Crabbe.'

'Miss Crabbe was an eccentric woman, Mr. Seaman,' was the reply, spoken by a tall, grave-looking man, who had the air of one who took life very seriously.

'She was very eccentric in her life, and, with a strange consistency, uncommon to her sex, she was eccentric in her death also. The saving clause in this will is that you were requested to hear it read, which looks to my mind as if her love for your little daughter were stronger than her love of conchology; and no doubt she hoped you would use all your influence to

B

induce Miss Poppy to fulfil the conditions by which she inherits the whole fortune.'

'If so, she was mistaken. Had I not heard the will, the probability is I should unconsciously have done so; now I shall remain perfectly neutral; and my impression is, Miss Crabbe knew that, and to make sure that no external influence should be brought to bear on the child, she ordered that I should hear the will read. I sincerely wish it were otherwise, not for the money's sake, but because I shall be so afraid of unconsciously fostering any taste for conchology in Poppy; and, on the other hand, it won't do for me to throw any obstacles in the way, because, in her state of health, an object of this kind is the very thing for her, and I deeply regret I shall feel in honour bound to appear perfectly neutral.'

'I see what you mean. It is a difficult position, no doubt. You clearly understand all the conditions, or shall I read it again?' said Mr. Seaman, pausing before he turned the key in the box which now contained the will.

'I understand, I think. Miss Crabbe has left her collection of shells to Poppy, to be given to her at once. On her twenty-first birthday, if she has from pure love of the science added only twenty shells to the collection, she is to inherit the whole of Miss Crabbe's fortune; if, on the other hand, she takes no interest in the shells—parts with them or takes no care of them—she is to receive a legacy of five hundred pounds, and the remainder of the fortune is left to some charities specified in the will. Is this right?'

'Quite; only Miss Poppy is to be distinctly told the shells were the joy and delight of her godmother's life, and they are now hers, to do absolutely as she likes with, and no hint as to any money being left is to be given her; she is to consider the shells her fortune. There are some valuable books on the subject which are to be sent with the shells; they will be a great help to her if she is inclined to study them, as I sincerely hope, for her own sake as well as for yours, she may be.'

'Thank you. And now I must be off, or I shall miss my train. You will see that the shells are carefully packed?'

'Of course. You may expect them at the end of the week, and I will send an experienced man to unpack them, otherwise they may be damaged, for they are very fragile; if any are injured in the journey they are to be replaced at the cost of the estate.'

'Quite so. Good-day,' said Mr. Merton, leaving the lawyer's office with even a graver face than usual; and as the train bore him to his home on the south coast, he thought over the will, and the probable disappointment of his little daughter—who had, much against her father's wish, been taught to consider herself as her godmother's heiress—when she was told all she had inherited was a collection of shells. The chances were she would want to sell them, and he must not raise any objection, though he knew by so doing she would forfeit a handsome fortune. It was most unlikely that she would study them, or attempt to add to their number. Had she been well and strong, like other girls, she might have taken it into her head, seeing that they

B 2

lived by the seaside, to go down to the beach and search
among the rocks and pools for other specimens; but she
had curvature of the spine, and for the next two or
three years she would be chained to her sofa, though
ultimately the doctors hoped she would outgrow the
disease and be able to get about. Then, again, she had
never shown any taste for natural history in any branch.
She was fond of reading, and she drew beautifully, in
spite of the recumbent position she was forced to
remain in. She was clever with her fingers, and did a
great deal of needlework of various kinds; but a hobby
such as this was quite out of her line, and her father
had not the faintest hope that she would take it up.

The short November day was closing in when Mr.
Merton drove up to the Rectory, for he was the rector
of Highcliff, and the great fire in the pretty low drawing-
room was very inviting after the cold raw air outside.
The hubbub of voices was evidently considered less
welcome to the master of the house, for it ceased when
he entered, and only one girlish voice, whose owner
knew she was a privileged person, was heard saying,

'Oh! Father, I am so glad you have come back; it
has seemed such a long day. Be quick and tell me all
about it; I am longing to know how rich I have grown
in a few days.'

The speaker was a girl apparently about seventeen
years of age. She was lying on a couch made on purpose
for her, which could be wheeled from room to room; a
rest for her books or drawing was attached to it, but
just now was pushed on one side. A long tawny mane,
with red lights in it, lay about the pillow, and a large

tress touched the ground; the fire-light fell full on her
face, which was lighted up with eager expectant joy at
her father's entrance. It was a pale face, and her name
of Poppy did not go well with it; but her brothers were
wont to tease her by saying the name referred to her
hair, which nevertheless was far from red, as they would
have been the first to grant. It was a young face, but
not so young as the girl, for pain and the confinement
of the last year had aged it. It was a sad face at times
though just now it was beaming with hope and eager
interest, but the monotonous life and constant pain had
subdued the natural high spirit and cast a deep shadow
over the gaiety of youth. It was a sweet face, for
neither suffering nor the deprivations she was forced to
submit to had yet soured the naturally sweet temper
and the smiles that played frequently about the lips
were a charming if a sad contrast to the look of pain in
the great brown eyes. It was a pretty face, as two of the
occupants of the room, to whom we will presently turn
our attention, seemed to think, for they looked at it very
often. Figure is never the strong point of girls of this
age, though some may show promising signs for the
future. It is a transition stage, and therefore far from a
beautiful period; but Poppy was just now encased in
plaster-of-paris, so that even if her recumbent position
had not hidden her figure, it would have been impossible
to judge what she was really like. One thing only was
certain, she was very tall, as the length of her couch
testified, and her long white fingers seemed to assert,
while the chances were in favour of her growing much
taller if she had to remain much longer on her back.

By her side sat a dark, handsome youth of seventeen or eighteen, holding a skein of wool which she was winding, and watching her with a mixed look of pity and admiration in his fine eyes. At the foot of her sofa sat another youth apparently the same age, but in reality he, Luke Thorne, was two or three years older than handsome Arthur Graham, though he was smaller and slighter and certainly by no means handsome. He had a book in his hand, but he was not reading, perhaps because the lamps were not yet lighted—perhaps he preferred to sit and watch the winding of the wool.

Two younger boys were lying at their mother's feet on the hearthrug, but they rose on their father's entrance and seated themselves, in the hope that they would be permitted to remain and hear about their sister's fortune.

'Well, father, what news have you for me? Please be quick and tell me, I am longing to know,' said Poppy, as her father took up a position on the hearthrug with his back to the fire.

'Let us have the lamps brought in first, my child. Robert, ring the bell. Edward, is your Latin done?'

'Latin and lamps, when I want to know how rich I am. Father, you are too cruel; isn't he, Arthur?' said Poppy, giving the ball of wool an impatient little pull which broke the strand.

Cruel or not, Mr. Merton did not vouchsafe to say a word on the subject of the will until the lamps were brought in, the shutters shut, and the curtains drawn; and then watching narrowly the effect of his words he said briefly:

'Poppy, your godmother has left you her most precious possession, a collection of shells.'

'Of shells! I wish it had been books; but go on, father, what else? How much money has she left me? I don't care about all the etceteras; it sounds very mercenary, I am afraid, but, oh! I do want to do such heaps of things with my money, not for myself, but for other people. How much am I to have, father?'

'My dear child, your fortune is this collection of shells, which I believe is very valuable, and which is to be sent to you in a few days; and you are to do absolutely as you like with it, remembering it was the joy of Miss Crabbe's heart and is the work of years.'

'Father! What do you mean? Are the shells all she has left me?'

'All except the trifling legacy of a few hundred pounds, five hundred I think it is, to be paid on your twenty-first birthday.'

'What an old humbug!' exclaimed Arthur Graham, who was evidently on intimate terms with the family.

'I call it a regular swindle of old Crabbe,' said Robert.

'Robert, leave the room this moment,' said his father sternly.

'I should sell the whole lot directly they arrived if I were you, Poppy,' said Edward.

'Go after your brother, sir, this instant. How dare you two boys express your opinion in this way?' said Mr. Merton hastily, as Edward followed his brother out of the room.

Poor Mr. Merton! Strict as he was with his boys, he was not usually snappish; but it certainly was provoking that Edward should, unconsciously, immediately suggest the very course which would deprive his sister of her fortune.

'What is the collection worth, George?' asked Mrs. Merton, apparently struck with Edward's advice.

'I don't know, I am sure; I understand it is a very good one. I believe she had over a thousand shells.'

'But shells are not valuable, are they?' said Poppy.

'Some are very valuable; the *Gloria maris*, for instance, is worth ten times its weight in gold, and two or three pounds is not at all a high price for a rare shell,' said Luke.

'And I suppose all hers are rare. Perhaps the collection is worth. at least a thousand pounds then,' said Poppy.

'My dear child, no, I don't think it can possibly be worth more than two or three hundred pounds at the outside; but I really don't know.'

'Well, I shall certainly sell it, if it is only worth two hundred pounds; that is better than nothing,' said Poppy.

'So should I; shells are such uninteresting things,' said Graham.

'I don't agree with you there, they are certainly very beautiful, and I think very interesting, little as I know of them. If I may make a suggestion, I should say wait till you see them, Poppy, before you decide to sell them,' said Luke Thorne; for which remark Mr. Merton inwardly blessed him.

'I may sell them if I like, mayn't I, father? Didn't you say I can do what I will with them?'

'Yes, dear, they are yours to do as you like with, to keep or sell; no one else has any right to object to anything you may decide on.'

'Well, don't you think yourself, father, shells are stupid things, and that the best thing I can do is to sell them? There are so many other things I would so much rather have.'

'I confess I have never thought them an interesting study, perhaps because I know nothing about them, but you see Luke says they are,' said Mr. Merton, evasively.

'Oh! Thorne thinks every nettle and every weed he comes across interesting, so I am not surprised to hear he thinks shells are. Let him and me sell them for you, Poppy; we'll get a good price for them; if Luke knows a little about them, he'll have an idea of their value,' said Graham.

'Very well, if father does not object; do you, father?'

'Not in the least; but I agree with Luke, I should see them before I decided what to do with them.'

'I will see them certainly before they are sold, but I have quite decided to sell them. They are utterly useless things to me. I can't think what made her leave me such a silly legacy, when she always said I was to inherit her fortune.'

'Crabbedness, mere crabbedness, nothing else,' said Graham.

'Perhaps she thought the study would interest you, Poppy; for my part I believe it would; there is an immense deal to learn about them; evidently the old lady found a great delight in them. I believe a hobby is a great source of happiness to most people; no doubt she thought if you took up the subject it might pass many a weary hour in a pleasant way for you. At any rate, I don't like to think that the old lady, who was certainly fond of you, deliberately chose her last action to be mere caprice or crabbedness, as Graham suggests. I think better of the human race in general, and of Miss Crabbe in particular, than that,' said Luke Thorne.

'Of course you do, we know you make the best of everybody and everything, even of crabby old maids, doesn't he, Mr. Merton?' said Graham.

But Mr. Merton had slipped out of the room during Luke's speech, for he was afraid he might betray by word or look some sign of the intense interest he could not help feeling in the fate of the shells. He was a poor man, with no means beyond his living, which was not a large one, though he supplemented it by taking one pupil, who always lived in the family, and economised it by educating his two boys himself. Luke Thorne was the present pupil, and he was reading theology before going up to college, preparatory to taking orders. Fortunately Mr. Merton was not blessed with a large family, he had but these three children; but poor little Poppy was more expense than three or four healthy children would have been; and Mr. Merton would have sacrificed his last penny, if necessary, rather than leave a stone unturned which might restore her to health and strength, for she was the darling of his heart. It was therefore a matter of almost vital importance to him that she should not forfeit the handsome fortune which was hers if only some one could inspire her with a love of shells. No wonder he felt strangely moved when he found Luke Thorne seemed rather inclined to do so, though every one else was disposed to urge her to sell the collection at once. Unfortunately, Luke had not, so her father thought, half as much influence over Poppy as handsome Arthur Graham, who was a sub-lieutenant in the Navy, and just now home on leave, though daily expecting a summons to join his ship. He was the only son of the squire of the parish, and already spent more of his time than his mother liked by the side of Poppy's couch, though she comforted herself by thinking Arthur was still only a boy, and Poppy a mere child; still, she was anxious about him, for she was an ambitious woman, and nothing would vex her more than what she privately described as an entanglement with a penniless cripple.

And yet Poppy was not exactly penniless, for this fortune was trembling in the balance; neither was she a cripple, for her doctors had every hope that in a year or two her spine would be quite straight, and she able to walk and get about. Nevertheless, from Mrs. Graham's point of view she was not a desirable wife for Arthur; and, as she shrewdly remarked, 'Although they were both too young to think of marrying or giving in marriage, still you never can tell what these childish friendships may lead to.'

'I'll tell you what it is, Poppy,' said Graham, when he found Mr. Merton had gone out of the room; 'it is no use wasting any time about these shells. The best way to sell them is to advertise; let us draw up an advertisement, and I'll send it off to-night to two or three papers.'

'But what will it cost?' said Poppy.

'It won't cost you anything. I'll pay for them, so that I may have the fun of receiving the answers; or if you are going to be proud and silly about them, we will deduct the expenses from the two hundred pounds. I don't myself believe they'll be worth a penny more than that.'

'It is quite possible they may, though,' interrupted Thorne.

'But not probable, I am afraid, Luke,' said Mrs. Merton sadly; for, truth to tell, the will was a great disappointment to her.

'It is quite impossible to judge of their value till we see them; but it must be a very poor collection if it would not realise more than that, though, of course, their intrinsic worth is not much; but why not wait till they come before advertising them for sale?' said Thorne.

'Simply because, my dear Thorne, I mean the advertisement to be in to-morrow's papers. I'll telegraph them, to make sure of it. Now, look here; listen. Will this do?' said Graham, who for the last few minutes had been scribbling in his pocket-book.

TO CONCHOLOGISTS. — For Sale immediately. A Magnificent Collection of Shells.

'What kind of shells? Marine or land shells, British

or foreign, fossil or of living species?' interrupted Thorne.

'How on earth are we to know that?'

'Simply by waiting till they arrive, when I shall be able to tell you,' said Thorne.

'Never mind. Shells will do; it includes all kinds of shells. The vaguer the information we give the better; we shall have all the more answers; it only piques the curiosity of the reader. Listen again. "A magnificent collection of shells. No reasonable offer refused. Communicate immediately with The Young Squire, Post Office, Highcliff." Will that do?'

'No! You have got "immediately" twice in two lines,' said Thorne, who disapproved of all this haste.

'Well, I'll strike out the last "immediately" and put "at once." Poppy, will it do now? Mrs. Merton, do you think it will do?'

'Yes, beautifully,' said Poppy and her mother in a breath.

'Then I'll be off at once and telegraph it to two or three of the papers; so good-bye.'

And the next morning, when Mr. Merton opened his paper, the first thing that caught his eye was Graham's advertisement to conchologists, which puzzled him greatly till Luke Thorne explained that Graham had telegraphed it up to town on the previous evening.

'Graham is too kind,' said Mr. Merton briefly; and somehow Luke suspected there was a hidden meaning in his words.

Luke knew his tutor well, and already he felt sure that, in spite of Mr. Merton's apparent indifference, he did not wish the shells to be sold. 'Now he has no love of natural science, so it can't be on that account that he wishes Poppy to keep them,' thought Luke. 'I wonder what his reason can be. Perhaps he thinks a hobby would be good for her; I am quite sure it would. Anyhow, I agree with Merton, it is a pity to sell them —for I am sure he thinks so, and I'll do all in my power to induce her to keep them, only, unfortunately, Graham will do all he can to persuade her to get rid of them, and Mrs. Merton and the boys will back him up, while Merton, I see, means to remain neutral. I wish the shells would come; perhaps when she sees them she will wish to keep them.'

But the shells were not expected till the end of the week, and before they arrived Graham came in one evening with a bundle of letters in his hand, which he threw on to Poppy's sofa.

'There, Poppy, there is a budget for you, all answers to my advertisement; we sha'n't have much difficulty in disposing of them as soon as we are in a position to answer some of the questions they ask. See, there are ten or a dozen people who want a list of all the shells contained in the collection. Now, Thorne, can you make one out the day they arrive?'

'Certainly not; if it is at all a large collection, it will take hours to do, even if every shell is labelled and if they are all classified; but most probably there will be a list sent with them, if so it can easily be copied.'

'Well, that part is soon settled; the next point is they all want us to name our price; now how are we to do that even when we see them? It won't do to sell them for a couple of hundred pounds, and then find out they were worth five hundred.'

'Oh no, that would be a great pity, would it not, father?' said Poppy.

'It would be unwise, I think,' was Mr. Merton's answer.

'It would be exceedingly foolish; why don't you decide to keep the shells till you know their value, Poppy?' said Luke.

'Nonsense, Luke; let her sell them at once; if she only gets a hundred pounds, a hundred pounds is a lot of money. I only wish I had it,' said Edward.

'I'd sell them for fifty pounds if they were mine; I don't believe they are worth that,' said Robert.

'You are both talking about what you don't understand in the least,' said Luke irritably.

'See, Poppy, some old lady encloses a list of the shells she wants; two or three seem open to buying single specimens. It would be much more trouble, but it is a question whether you would not make more money if you sold them separately. If I were going to remain here for the winter, I would arrange it all for you, and should like the work, but you see I may be ordered off at any moment, so unless Mr. Merton or Luke would manage it for you, I think we had better decide to sell the entire collection.'

'What do you think I had better do, father?' said Poppy.

'My dear child, I would much rather that you did not ask my advice in the matter at all. I wish you to do exactly as you like; but do not look to me to sell them separately for you, as that would involve a great deal of letter writing, and, as you know, this half-hour is the only spare time I have in the day. Perhaps Luke would undertake to see to them for you, if you decide to sell them separately, which I should say is the more profitable way.'

Now Luke was well known to be Poppy's most devoted slave; he fetched and carried for her at her bidding; her slightest wish was his law; everything that interested her interested him. He was never weary of devising means to amuse her; he would get up early and sit up late to make up for the time he spent by her sofa; indeed, it was well known he was quite capable of sacrificing himself to any extent for her sake; therefore no one in the room doubted that he would at once agree to sell the shells separately, no matter how much trouble it gave him. But to the surprise of every one he declined to do this, at any rate for the present.

'No, sir, I won't promise to have anything to do with the sale of the shells at all. I think it is a very great pity they are to be sold, and I am sure when they arrive Poppy and every one else will agree with me.'

'You are very unkind to me about these shells, Mr. Thorne,' said Poppy.

And her words pricked Luke as sharply as she intended; but he had the consolation of knowing he was right, and that was some salve to the wound.

CHAPTER II.

A PEEP AT THE COLLECTION.

'O Lord, how manifold are Thy works! in wisdom hast
Thou made them all: the earth is full of Thy riches.
'So is this great and wide sea, wherein are things creeping
innumerable, both small and great beasts.'—PSALM CIV. 24, 25.

> 'Ye swift-finned nations, that abide
> In seas as fathomless as wide,
> And unsuspicious of a snare
> Pursue at large your pleasures there,
> Poor sportive fools! how soon doth man
> Your heedless ignorance trepan.'—COWPER.

ON the Saturday morning after Mr. Merton's visit to
his lawyer, a furniture van drove up to the Rectory,
much to the disturbance of the boys' lessons; for the
study was in the front of the house, and after two or
three ineffectual attempts to keep their attention Mr.
Merton was obliged to let them go; and indeed there
was so much bustle and noise going on in the house,
that it was not easy to go on with Greek verbs and
Latin grammar.

In the first place, a rearrangement of the drawing-
room was necessary, to find room for the three handsome

C

cabinets which contained the shells; then the study
had to be invaded, and a long shelf cleared and given up
to the conchological library ; and finally a large packing-
case, which contained shells too large to go inside
the cabinets, was brought in and unpacked by a man
sent on purpose, and who begged, as a special favour,
that the young lady might not see the shells until he
had arranged them all in their proper order, a work
which took him several hours; so it was not till the
afternoon that Poppy was wheeled into the drawing-
room by Luke Thorne, who was still rather in her black
books; the rest of the family followed, for Mr. Merton
had forbidden any one to catch a glimpse of the
collection till it was unpacked, and had controlled his
own curiosity likewise ; for indeed he was very curious
both to see the shells and to see their effect on Poppy.

'Three cabinets! And are they all full of shells?'
was Poppy's first exclamation.

'Yes, miss, every drawer is as full as it can be; but
there is another cabinet, if you should care to enlarge the
collection, which I believe Miss Crabbe hoped you would
do,' said the man, who probably had his own reasons
for hoping the collection was to be added to.

'Enlarge it, indeed! she is going to sell it, and she
ought to get a good sum for it too,' said Robert, going
up to one of the cabinets.

'Don't touch anything, Robert,' said Mr. Merton,
sharply.

'It is one of the finest private collections in
England, but if the young lady wishes to sell it, my
master would, I know, give a thousand pounds for it.

Miss Crabbe refused to let him have it for that some years ago, and it is worth more than that, though some shells have depreciated in value.'

'Indeed, how is that?'

'Well, sir, here is this Wentle Trap; years ago seventy guineas were given for a single specimen; you can get one now for seven-and-six. This specimen is worth more, for it is a very fine one,' said the man, taking up a small turreted white shell with many whorls, each whorl ornamented with numerous longitudinal bands, each band being the lip of a former mouth.

'Oh! the Precious Wentle Trap, *Scalaria pretiosa*. I know it well, it comes from the seas of China and Japan,' said Luke Thorne.

'Why is it called a Wentle Trap? does it catch wentles? and if so, what are wentles?' asked Robert.

'It is a corruption of the German name, *Wendeltreppe*, or winding staircase; the genus is supposed to resemble a staircase, hence the Latin name, *Scalaria*, a ladder or staircase,' said Luke.

'You understand shells, sir? Do you know this one?' said the man, turning to Luke as he opened another drawer and pointed to a long conical-shaped shell of remarkable beauty of shape, colour, and markings; the ground was white, with delicate dull red triangular lines all over it, and three broad bands of beautiful tints encircling it.

'*Gloria maris*, as I am alive! Poppy, you are a highly favoured mortal indeed. Do you know there are only twelve known specimens of this shell in the world? and you actually possess one of the twelve. Oh! it

c 2

would be wicked to talk of selling this shell!' exclaimed Luke enthusiastically.

'I don't see very much in it; I would much rather have one of these big shells on the top of the cabinet,' said Edward.

'That Glory of the Sea was the glory of Miss Crabbe's life, sir; it is practically priceless. She had this secret drawer made on purpose for it. I will show the young lady how it goes before I leave; and this cabinet has always been kept locked.'

'There is a story of a Frenchman who years ago possessed the only *Gloria maris* then in the world, except one which belonged to a Dutchman. When the Dutchman died his specimen was put up to auction; the Frenchman outbid every one, and then crushed it beneath his heel and exclaimed, "Now my specimen is the only one,"' said Luke.

'What sublime selfishness!' said Arthur Graham, who had entered the room while Thorne was speaking. 'Hulloa, Poppy, you seem to have inherited a museum; these are shells indeed,' he continued, pointing to the large shells on the top of the cabinet which had already attracted Robert's attention.

And here it may be observed that it was one of Mr. Merton's peculiarities not to allow his boys' names to be shortened to Bobby or Ted. He considered it was right that people should be called by their baptismal names, though he had been cajoled into allowing his daughter's name of Agatha to be altered into Poppy; but then exceptions to all his rules were made in favour of her.

'This is the Giant Clam, *Tridacna gigas*,' said the

man, taking an enormous bivalve shell in his hands and opening it, showing its beautiful opaque white interior. 'This is only an ordinary-sized specimen; they sometimes grow to an enormous size, and are said to weigh as much as five hundred pounds.'

'Two of them are used for holy water in the church of St. Sulpice, Paris, which were given to Francis the First by the Republic of Venice, and it is said that a hundred people could dine off the animal it comes from the Indian Ocean,' said Thorne.

'I don't believe it is ever large enough to dine a hundred people; at least, I should be sorry to be one of the hundred,' said Edward, with the charming candour of his species.

'Perhaps you don't believe the shell is sometimes so large that one person can with difficulty lift one of the valves : all the same, it is true. That is a Fountain Shell, *Strombus gigas*, Poppy; next to *Tridacna*, it is one of the largest living species,' said Luke.

'And this is a very good specimen, sir, it weighs nearly five pounds; they use these shells at Santa Cruz for paving the streets, they tell me, and in Europe they are used for making cameos. Occasionally pearls are found in them; a pink pearl weighing twenty-four grains was once found in a Fountain Shell, while the animal was being cleaned for table in the West Indies, where these large ones are mostly found.'

'What is that large oblong univalve, so beautifully coloured ?' asked Mr. Merton.

'A Triton, sir, *Triton variegatus;* it is a foot and a half long, a magnificent specimen; it is found on the

Asiatic coast, and in the Mediterranean and South Seas. They are called Conch shells, and are used in foreign countries as instruments of music; they bore a hole near the apex and blow through it, and thus produce musical notes.'

'To be sure; the ancient Greeks used to use them for a trumpet for the town crier, and I believe some nations used them as military horns; and I am afraid, Poppy, that is almost the extent of my conchology,' said Mr. Merton, who was sitting by his little girl's sofa, watching the wonder depicted on her face as she gazed speechlessly on her new possessions.

'Here is a great big shell like a helmet,' said Edward.

'It is a Helmet shell, sir, *Cassis tuberosa*; this shell is often used for engraving cameos, because of its pure delicate colour, and a considerable trade is carried on on the Continent with ornaments made from them.'

'Whereabouts do they carve the cameos?' said Robert.

'Why, on this beautiful enamel part by the mouth of the shell; the mantle which lines the interior rises in folds here, do you see, and secretes enamel; on this they carve their cameos,' said Luke.

'What do you mean by the mantle?'

'You must get Luke to explain that to you another day, Robert; we have only time now to take a hasty glance at the collection, so that we may have some little idea of what it contains.'

'There is a beautiful shell like a great ear, with holes perforated down one side; it looks as if it were made of mother-of-pearl, its colours are so beautiful; I should like to know something about that, please,' said Poppy finding her voice at last.

'It is the Ear shell, miss, *Haliotis*; the outside has been scraped to discover the nacre; it is generally very rough in these shells, but the inside is in its natural state, and shows all the colours of the rainbow. It is not a rare shell; in the Channel Islands they call these shells Ormers; they are very plentiful there, and the animal is used largely for food—they are well beaten first, to make them tender. This is not the same species as the Guernsey one, *Tuberculata*, but that has just as beautiful a shell inside as this one. I can show you several. There is a very long species, called the Ass's Ear. They all have these holes in one side; and perhaps this good gentleman will tell you what they are for.'

'They are made by the animal as it grows, some conchologists say, to allow the lobes of the mantle to pass through, as the creature increases in size; others say they are to let in water to the breathing organs through a slit in the mantle; probably they serve both purposes. The hinder ones are often closed as a new one is made, so that not more than seven or eight are open at a time; see, two or three are closed in this specimen. Sea Ear is its proper English name. No doubt Robert and Edward can tell us its derivation,' said Luke, who was rather given to teasing the boys.

'*Halios*, marine, and *ous*, an ear; they eat that creature in Japan. I have tasted it,' said Graham; 'isn't that a Nautilus up there?' he continued.

'Yes, sir, *Nautilus Pompilius*, and a lovely thing it is; see what an exquisite shape it is.'

'It is indeed; it used to be dedicated to the Egyptian priestess Arsinoë, and the ancients used it for a drinking-cup: the inside is lined with pearl, isn't it? Aristotle mentions this Pearly Nautilus, and the Paper Nautilus also, and describes them very well,' said Mr. Merton.

'Yes; only he represents them as floating on the sea in fine weather, and spreading out their arms to the breeze, like a sail, and the poets ever since have delighted in repeating the fable, hence Pope,

> "Learn of the little Nautilus to sail,
>   Spread the thin oar, and catch the driving gale."

But the Nautilus has neither oars to spread nor sails to catch the gale with. It does float on the sea when the waves become calm after a storm, with its head above water and its tentacles spread out on the surface, the shell being undermost and almost hidden. It has the power of sinking its shell by merely drawing in its tentacles, and then down it goes to its favourite spot at the bottom of the sea; but to say that it either rows or sails is nonsense.'

'No, Luke, only poetical license,' said Mr. Merton, smiling. 'I believe Pliny is great on the Nautilus, as well as Aristotle, and it was a Dutch merchant in the eighteenth century who first found out its power of sinking and rising. He discovered also that when they are at the bottom of the sea they creep along with their shell above them and their head and tentacles on the ground, in the reverse position to that which they assume when floating; they can go along pretty quickly, but often get entangled in the fishermen's nets.'

'I wish some of our fishermen here would land one at Highcliff one fine day,' said Robert.

'Here! Why, there are no *Nautili* in England. *Pompilius* comes from the warm seas of Asia, Australia, and the East and West Indies,' said Luke.

'Show us the Paper Nautilus, please,' said Poppy.

'There is not one, strange to say, in the collection, miss; it must have been an oversight of Miss Crabbe's, for it is one of the most beautiful shells, though very fragile when exposed to the air, but pliable enough in the water, or else it could not escape destruction.'

'Why, if it is anything like this Pearly Nautilus, I should think it would stand a good deal of knocking about,' said Graham.

'But it is not in the least like it; *Argonauta Argo*, or the Paper Nautilus—'

'Excuse me, Thorne, one moment. Boys, what is the English of *Argonautai?*'

'Sailors of the ship Argo,' said Graham promptly, to save Robert and Edward from making a blunder, which was the probable result of their efforts at replying.

'It is sometimes called the Paper Sailor; its shell is very thin and elastic, pure white and translucent, of a beautifully symmetrical fluted shape, containing only one chamber, whereas the home of the Nautilus contains from thirty to forty chambers. The Argonaut is very loosely, if at all, attached to its shell, which is not mounted on the body of the animal, but seems chiefly intended to serve the purpose of a cradle, for inside it the female

Argonaut lays her eggs. For a long time it was supposed that the animal in the shell was a parasite, who had appropriated this beautiful house to itself, but a Madame Power, then living at Messina, kept a number of Argonauts of all sizes in a tank and watched them, and discovered that when the young Argonauts were twelve days old they began with their two front arms to form a thin filmy layer of shell-like matter, which slowly but surely developed and hardened into a perfect shell. She also discovered that if the shell is broken the clever little Argonaut can repair it. It no more sails than the Nautilus ; indeed, it is doubtful if it ever floats, for its favourite haunts are deep water, where it swims by ejecting water from its funnel. It crawls in the same way as the Nautilus, with its shell over its back like a snail.'

'I wish I had one, I should so like to see it,' said Poppy.

'Where is it to be found, Thorne? Perhaps I may come across one some day; if I do I'll secure it for you, Poppy,' said Graham.

'There is not much use in doing that if the collection is to be sold. But it is not a rare species; the Mediterranean is a very good place for it, the Cape is another, and in any warm seas almost you might find it ; but it is so fragile, I doubt if it will arrive safely,' said Thorne.

'Oh yes, it will, sir, if it is carefully packed; it is not so fragile as these shells, the Sea Snail, *Ianthina*,' said the man opening a drawer and showing some little violet snail-like shells, which he promptly stopped

Robert from touching, assuring him they were so brittle the least roughness would break them; but he took out the drawer and handed it to Poppy.

'How pretty they look in their bed of pink cotton wool!' said Poppy.

'They are all packed and kept in cotton wool, some small ones are in little boxes, and the tiniest are gummed on to glass,' said the man, opening drawer after drawer, and showing shells of all sizes, beginning with some not much larger than a pin's head.

'Those *Ianthinæ* can emit a phosphorescent light, Poppy, and the animal gives out a violet fluid, which stains the hand. Whole fleets of the *Ianthinæ* are seen floating in calm weather in the South Atlantic, for their home is the high sea, and sometimes hundreds get wrecked on the coral-reefs; they stick to each other sometimes in a mass, like bees. They are some of the very few Molluscs which inhabit the ocean and yet have fragile shells, but yet they ride securely upon the waves, and make rapid progress. Now, it is possible you boys might find one of them here, for they sometimes drift to our southern and western coasts. Let me put that drawer back, Poppy, and we'll have another out.'

'These are the Cowries, miss,' said the man, handing Poppy a drawer of thick glossy shells of vivid colours and delicate markings, 'one of which—the Tiger Cowry —is known to everybody.'

'You have not *Princeps* and *Leucodon*, I suppose?' said Luke.

'No, sir. They are in the National Collection, but

they are unique, and perhaps the most valuable shells yet discovered. There is the Money Cowry, *Cyprœa moneta*.'

'Why is it called the Money Cowry?' asked Robert.

'Because it is used by the natives of West Africa as money; it is the current coin, too, of Siam and Bengal. The negro women collect it, and it is sent to the different countries. In 1848 sixty tons of Money Cowries were imported into Liverpool, and then exported for coin into Africa. This used to be done annually, and may be to this day, for aught I know. But now, Edward, I have explained the meaning of *moneta*, do you know what *Cyprœa* means?' said Mr. Merton.

'No. I know Cypris is one of the names for Venus——'

'Right! *Cyprœa* is the Greek for Venus, and I suppose the name has been given to these shells on account of their beauty.'

'What is this white shell with bright orange teeth called?' asked Poppy.

'The Orange Cowry. It is a rare one. The chiefs of the Friendly Isles wear it as an ornament; it is a badge of rank. But still rarer is *Cyprœa aurora*. Yes, you have one. Look! I know it by this hole, which was pierced by some New Zealander; it is not a natural perforation; they suspend it to their dress as an ornament. That one there, *Annulus*, is used for money, for ornament, and to weight their fishing-nets with, by the West Indians.'

'Are any of the Cowries found in England?' asked Poppy.

'The Nun Cowry is very common; but it is small and

not at all remarkable for beauty; it is a dull brown. See, there are some Nuns; none of the European species have brilliant tints. Let us have the Pectens next— they are some of the prettiest shells. See! There is a blaze of colour for you, Poppy,' said Luke, as a drawer of Pectens was pulled out.

'I call those Scallops,' said Edward.

'So they are; but *Pecten* is their family name. It means comb, Poppy. *Pecten Jacobœus*, or St. James's shell. Here he is; used to be worn by the pilgrims to the Holy Land. It is the scallop-shell that we hear so much of. Like the pilgrims, the scallops are great travellers, and sometimes get deserted by the tide, and then what do you think they do? They jump back. They take a series of leaps till they get back to the sea. They can go about half a foot at a leap, and they do it by expanding their valves, and then closing them with a jerk. Besides this, they can lie at anchor in a storm. They spin a thread, and by it moor themselves to a rock or boulder, and there they lie safely till the storm is over, otherwise they might be dashed against the rocks by the force of the waves and their shells broken, for they prefer shallow water near the shore. There are nine British species; I wonder if you have them all, Poppy?'

'No, sir; I think only four. Miss Crabbe's collection is chiefly foreign and very rare shells. I believe she thought the commoner kinds could be added at any time. I dare say you would find several of the Pectens on the beach, and they are all very pretty; but they don't equal *Spondylus*, the Thorny Oyster. There are some beautiful specimens of that genus; it belongs to the same family as the Pectens, and is by far the most beautiful of all the bivalves.'

'Oh! what lovely things—red and pink and yellow and orange. Oh! father, just look! Aren't they exquisite?' said Poppy, as another drawer of thorny bivalves, of vivid colours, was placed on her sofa.

'They are indeed, Poppy. I remember my old friend Aristotle was struck with their beauty. I don't suppose we shall find anything prettier than these in the collection. Where do they come from, Luke?'

'The Indian Ocean and the Mediterranean, sir. There is another shell still more beautiful in form than *Spondylus*—the *Murex*. Will you show us that next, please?'

'We call that sort of shell the Sting Winkle. There are plenty of the common ones on the beach, and the fishermen say they make holes in the shells of other fish with their spines,' said Robert.

'You don't find any like these on the beach, I am sure, Robert,' said Luke, as he put a drawer of exquisitely coloured univalves of singularly beautiful shape, and armed with long spines, which added greatly to their beauty, on Poppy's sofa.

'That is Venus's Comb, *Murex tenuispina*; when the animal wants to enlarge its shell, it can dissolve those spines and replace them with a smooth surface. This one, *Trunculus*, yields a purple dye,' said the packer.

'Tyrian purple; the Romans are said to have obtained this colour from the juice of the *Murex*, which was found on the shores of Tyre; and there is an old legend which says it was discovered by a shepherd's dog, which broke one of the shells on the beach, and stained his mouth with the colour. They bruised the shells in mortars to extract the dye; and heaps of these broken shells, and holes in the rocks, which were evidently used for coppers, may still be seen on the Tyrian shores,' said Mr. Merton.

'Why, father, you said you knew nothing about shells; why, you know more than any of us except Luke.'

'But we none of us know anything, so that isn't much of a compliment to Luke, Poppy,' said Edward.

'I don't know much, but I mean to learn a good deal, if Poppy does not sell the books as well as the shells on Monday,' said Luke.

'I never said I was going to sell them on Monday!' said Poppy indignantly. 'I am certainly going to look at them all first, and I have not seen half yet.'

'No; we must get on quicker, if you please, sir. I should like to show the young lady just the principal shells before I go. These are the Harps: there is the *Imperialis;* it is very rare, it comes from the Mauritius, it is a very beautiful shell, and used to fetch an enormous price, but it is not so scarce or so dear now; there is a fishery for them at the Mauritius; there are only nine species, and perhaps this one, *Ventricosa,* which is as common as any, is the most beautiful.'

'Yes, I think it is; see, Poppy, how symmetrical all these ribs, which represent the strings of the harp, are; each of those ribs was formerly a *varix,* or vein. I believe the animals which inhabit the Harps are very beautiful, and of brilliant colours, rosy red and yellowish green. Now, these are the Cones coming next; we have seen the most rare of them, *Gloria maris*,' said Thorne.

'We have the Field of the Cloth of Gold here, sir, and a lovely thing it is; no brocade made by human hands can equal the exquisite design on that shell; and here is the *Imperialis*. See the elaborate painting of these yellow and brown bands, and the number of lovely shades used in the work; others have markings like Greek and Hebrew letters, and others are marked with dots, veins, clouds, stripes, bands; every kind of decoration seems to be employed. There are over three hundred species of *Conus*, and there are two hundred species in this collection. Here is one, *Cedo Nulli*, you would not get for less than seven or eight pounds. They come chiefly from Asia, but they are abundant in all tropical seas, and I believe are generally found in the holes of rocks and caves.'

'Are there no British specimens?' asked one of the boys.

'No; and it is lucky for you there are not, for some species bite when handled. Here we come to the Mitres. They are as numerous as the Cones—I mean they have as many species. Some are very minute, and they are all slender and elegant in form. Here is *Episcopalis*. My lord can give out a purple liquid with a disagreeable odour when irritated, and some species are said to be poisonous, and if touched will wound with their pointed trunk—not a dignified use for a bishop to put his mitre to, is it? They are exquisitely moulded; sometimes grooved, sometimes fluted, sometimes smooth,' said Luke.

'Are these British ?'

'None of these. They are mostly from the Pacific; but there are a great many fossil species found in our chalk. Here is a quaint shell, young gentlemen, often found on the Norfolk coast, where it is very common— the Razor Shell. See, it is a bivalve; but enormously long in proportion to its breadth, for bivalves are measured in this way : from the hinge to the margin is called the breadth, from posterior side to the anterior side the length. If you have any *Solens* on this coast, you must look for them at low water, for they live buried in the sand. You can discover their where-abouts by a mark like a keyhole in the sand, and you may perhaps catch them with a piece of bent wire, and they are very good to eat when cooked. They never come out of their holes of their own will, and sometimes sink to a depth of one or two feet. They are more curious than beautiful.

'There is another way of catching them I know of. Put a little salt down their holes; that irritates them, and up they'll come. Then you must be quick and snatch at them, for, if you miss them, they won't come up a second time—they are too knowing for that. Here, in this drawer, we have the Fool's Cap Limpet (*Capulus*). See, the shape is very like a fool's cap; the very large species are tropical, but one, called the Hungarian Cap, is found in our British seas. Here it is, look; white outside, lined with a beautiful rose colour. It is supposed that the animals never move from the spot they originally settle upon. Now we come to the Needle Shells. By the way, Poppy, I hope

D

you don't think we are going through these shells in any sort of order, because we are not; we are just taking those which are the most attractive at first sight, just to give you a general idea of what they are like.'

'Yes, and we must not spend more time over them to-day; so if you have anything to say about the Needle Shells, be quick please, Luke, and say it,' said Mr. Merton.

'They get their name from their sharp-pointed form. They are tropical, excepting one which is found in the Mediterranean, and some species are ten inches long. They love the sea, and seldom get out of its reach. There! I could spend hours talking about them,' said Luke enthusiastically, as the cabinets were closed.

'So you may another day; but now will you all go out of the room for a minute, while the packer shows Poppy how this secret drawer goes? I had better see it also, Poppy, in case you forget,' said Mr. Merton.

So the boys and Mrs. Merton went away while the secret of the drawer which contained *Gloria maris* was explained.

When they all came back, Poppy exclaimed :

'I feel like the Queen of Sheba when she had been looking at all King Solomon's treasures; there is no more spirit in me.'

'Well, you have no need to feel like her. Her spirit was taken out of her, because the treasures were Solomon's, and not hers. Now, your shells are your own,' said Graham.

'Until she sells them!' said Luke, in a tone which was meant to be reproving, but was taken to be unkind; for Poppy made no answer, but burst into tears.

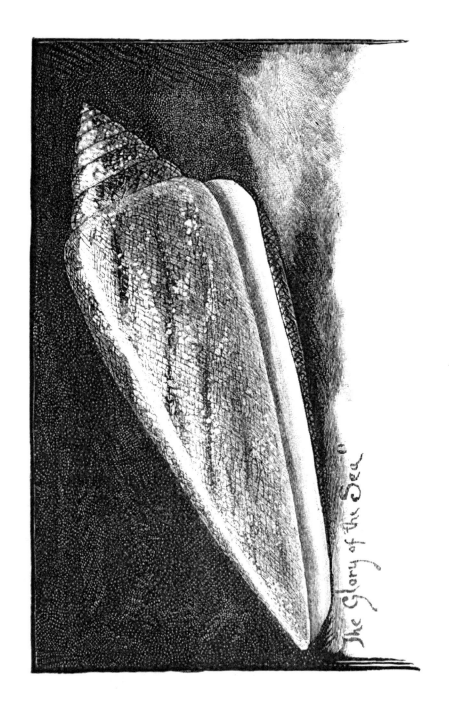

The Glory of the Sea

CHAPTER III.

'GLORIA MARIS' IS LOST.

'But be ye glad and rejoice for ever in that which I create.'—
ISAIAH LXV. 18.

'Master, I marvel how the fishes live i' the sea.'
'Why, as men do a-land; the great ones eat up the little ones.
—*Pericles.* SHAKSPEARE.

AN awkward silence, broken only by Poppy's sobs,
followed Luke Thorne's remark; in the midst of which
he rose abruptly and left the room.

'Poppy, dear, you are over-tired; the excitement of
these shells arriving has been too much for you,' said
Mrs. Merton.

'It is not that so much, Mrs. Merton; it is Thorne's
temper. He has been as cross and as rude to Poppy as
he could be ever since we spoke of selling the shells;
they are hers to do as she likes with, and if she chooses
to sell them it has nothing to do with Thorne. It is
great cheek of him to interfere, I consider,' said Graham
savagely.

'It is just like Luke; he likes to manage us all,
Poppy, as well as us boys,' said Robert.

'Never mind, Poppy; we know a little about their value now from that man. By the way, he told me by far the best plan is not to sell the entire collection, but to sell the shells separately; it takes much longer, but in the end you will realise almost as much again.'

'But I don't want to sell them at all,' sobbed Poppy.

'Don't want to sell them!' exclaimed the two boys in a breath.

'Not sell them! What are you going to do with them then?' asked Graham.

'I don't think she knows what she wants, Arthur; she has done too much, poor child,' said Mrs. Merton.

'Perhaps I'd better be off, then. Come on, you fellows; I'll take you for a walk before tea, if Mr. Merton does not object.'

Mr. Merton made no objection. On the contrary, he was very glad when Mrs. Merton followed the boys out of the room and left him alone with Poppy; for her remark that she did not want to sell the shells, when for the last few days, until within the last hour, she had talked of little else but selling them, had filled him with curiosity to know what the meaning of this sudden change was, and he felt sure Poppy, with a very little encouragement, would tell him. Under ordinary circumstances he would have been at her side at the first sign of tears, and asked what they meant, but he was afraid to evince any anxiety in the fate of the shells, lest he should in any way influence her to keep them; so he had held aloof, thereby increasing Poppy's grief, and making her think he was angry with her as well as

Luke. As soon as they were alone Mr. Merton went across the room, and sitting down by Poppy's sofa, bent over and kissed her.

'What is the matter, my child? I don't think Luke meant to be unkind.'

'No, but he is angry with me, and I thought you were too.'

'But you see I am not in the least angry; why should I be?'

'Because I was so mercenary about those shells; I was so disappointed when I heard Miss Crabbe had only left me them, and no money.'

'It was a great disappointment, no doubt, my darling; older people than you would have felt that. I own I did, so I can't be angry with you for that.'

'But I was cross with poor dead Miss Crabbe, and I hated the shells, and longed to sell them; and now I have seen them I think she must have been very fond of me, or she would never have left such treasures to me, for they are so beautiful. I am sure she must have been very fond of them, and I think I ought to take great care of them for her sake. I think they are a sort of trust; so if you don't mind, father, I should like to keep them; it seems to me, now I have seen them, it would be almost a sin to sell such lovely things; don't you think it would?'

Mr. Merton hesitated before he answered. He was secretly intensely relieved to find Poppy inclined to keep the shells, but he was dreadfully afraid of letting her see his relief.

'No, dear, I don't think it would be a sin to sell

them, but I am just as well pleased that you should keep them, and I like your motive for doing so.'

'But it is not all a good motive. I like having things that very few other people have, and that is selfish, isn't it? But then I like these shells for their beauty, as well as for their rarity, and I begin to long to hear more about them; where they all come from, what kind of animals lived in such beautiful homes, and how they make such lovely houses for themselves.'

'That I can't tell you, dear; all I know is God, who made them, taught them also how to build their beautiful houses as a protection. He might have been content with giving them something far less beautiful, which would, perhaps, have served the purpose as well, but He chose to make them beautiful also. He has taught these creatures to be sculptors and artists, and I cannot help thinking He did this for our benefit; that in admiring these exquisite shapes and lovely colours, we might be led to think of His perfect beauty. I love to think that we were in the Creator's thoughts when He made the lower animals, and that He made them not only to be our food, and our servants, but to be our teachers, our joy, and delight also. In the first instance, He made them all for Himself, we are told; but no doubt their secondary purpose was to minister to man; and not merely to satisfy his physical hunger, but to stimulate his love of science, and above all to increase his love of God, to minister to his body, soul, and spirit. I believe no one has yet fathomed the mystery of how the shell is made, but no doubt Luke will be able to tell you more about it,' said Mr. Merton.

'He could if he chose, but he is so angry with me for wishing to sell the shells, I am afraid he won't.'

'And I am sure he will; but I think I must forbid him to talk of them any more to-day, as you are too exhausted with all this excitement. I will suggest to him that on Monday he shall begin regularly to give you lessons in conchology, if you like.'

Poppy was delighted with this proposition, and Luke, who did not appear again till tea-time, was no less so when Mr. Merton suggested it, for he had been abusing himself in the interim for being an ill-tempered brute, who had interfered in what did not concern him, and hurt the feelings of a poor little invalid girl, who, young as she was, he already loved with all the ardour of first love, though he managed to conceal his feelings so well that no one suspected their existence. Indeed, Poppy's extreme youth, and her state of health, quite prevented Mr. or Mrs. Merton from suspecting that either Luke or Arthur Graham looked upon her in any other light than that of a delicate child, whom it was a charity to amuse. And yet, as Thorne had discovered, Graham too was devoted to Poppy, and, with his wealthy position and handsome face, was likely to prove a formidable rival, when the child was old enough to think about lovers.

She did not join the family party at tea that night, but remained, by her mother's orders, quietly alone in the drawing-room, whither Luke sought her as soon as he could make an excuse for leaving the table.

'Poppy, I was very ill-tempered and unkind to you—' began Luke.

'No, you weren't, I was silly to cry,' interrupted Poppy.

'Yes, I was; you said so yourself, and it was true; but if you'll forgive me I'll make up for it by teaching you the little I know, and a great deal more, for I'll study some of those books of yours about shells. Is it a bargain?'

'Oh, thank you, thank you, Luke!' said Poppy, radiant with joy, as she put one of her long white hands into Luke's.

Luke Thorne was certainly not handsome; but he was a neat dapper little man, with small hands and feet, firmly closed lips and resolute grey eyes. There was plenty of character, if there was no beauty, in his face, and they seldom go together, for character as a rule destroys the balance and turns the scales in its own favour. But as he took Poppy's hand and raised it almost reverently to his lips to seal their bargain he looked by no means ugly, for pity, love, sympathy, reverence and penitence were all written on his ordinary features, illuminating them with a grace mere physical beauty often lacks.

Mrs. Merton's entrance put an end to the little scene, and by Mr. Merton's wish no more was said about the shells that day, and Sunday was such a busy day at the Vicarage, what with services and Sunday school classes, that there was no time to think of them; but on Monday afternoon Luke came into the drawing-room to tea and to give Poppy her first lesson in conchology.

'Poppy, I have been asking Mr. Merton if I may

give a lecture at our first penny-reading this year, in the schoolroom, and he says Yes; now what do you think the subject is to be?'

'Shells, Luke; I am sure you have not another idea in your head just now.'

'Right! Well, now in this lecture I shall try and tell you a little about the habits, structure and physiology of the Mollusca, as this sub-kingdom is called; it includes all soft-bodied animals enveloped in a muscular skin, and generally living in a shell, and is derived from the Latin word *mollis*, soft. The lecture will contain general information on the ways and appearances of shells and their inhabitants; but you want particular information, so in these lessons I want to go straight through the classes, families, and in some cases genera, and occasionally even species of shells, taking a glance at your specimens to illustrate what would otherwise be far less interesting. By this means we shall find out what shells are wanting to make the collection perfect, and which of those it would be most interesting to have. Well, now to start off, the classes into which the Mollusca are divided are——'

'Wait a minute, Luke. I believe I know that; there are two classes, aren't there—univalves and bivalves?'

'Those are divisions, and, as you know, all shells consisting of only one piece—like a snail, or a cone, or a cowry—are called univalves; all consisting of two valves or shells—like the mussel, or scallop, or oyster— are called bivalves. These divisions are again divided into five classes—first, *Cephalopoda*, or head-footed, so called because the animal has arms or feet arranged in a circle round its mouth; the name is derived from two Greek words—*cephal*, a head, and *poda*, feet. The second class is *Gasteropoda*, from *gaster*, the under side of the body, so called because the animal walks on the under side of its body, which forms the foot, as the snail, for instance. The third class is *Pteropoda*, from *pteron*, a wing; these creatures swim with a pair of fins, or wings extending on each side of the head; they are entirely marine animals. These three classes are all univalves, and the animals all have heads; the remaining classes are bivalves, and the animals are acephalous— that is, they have no heads.'

'No heads, Luke? What queer creatures they must be!'

'You would think an oyster with a head still queerer, wouldn't you? The fourth class is called *Brachiopoda*, from *brachion*, an arm; they have two long, spiral arms near their mouth—for they have a mouth, though they have no head—and with these arms, which they can unroll, they make currents, which help to convey their food into their mouths. The fifth class is the *Conchifera*, or shell-bearers, the ordinary bivalve, like the oyster; these creatures breathe by two pairs of gills attached to the mantle.'

'Oh! Please tell me what you mean by the mantle?'

'It is an outer skin which envelops the animal entirely, and from it exudes a liquid, which, when exposed to the air or water, hardens into the shell—in other words, the mantle is an envelope or covering which secretes the shell; in the univalves it takes the form of a sac, in bivalves it is divided into two lobes— one lobe for each valve.'

'How is it that only the inside of shells have that beautiful mother-of-pearly look ?'

'Nacreous, Poppy; not mother-of-pearly. Why is the lining nacreous ? Because that is formed by the thin transparent part of the mantle which contains the viscera; the epidermis, or outer layer, and the cellular parts are formed by the margin or collar of the mantle. Every layer of a shell was once a portion of the mantle, and then, having been hardened with carbonate of lime, was thrown off to join itself to those layers previously formed; but the exact way in which this outer shell is made is a mystery.'

'Where do they get the carbonate of lime from ?'

'Oh, from their food. There is abundance of lime in land plants, which land molluscs feed on, and seaweed contains a great deal of lime, for it collects it from the salt water, to which it acts as a filter; there is no scarcity of lime for them, witness the enormous thickness of some of their shells, which means they have too much lime in their systems. How this lime is built up into the wonderful cellular structures is, as I said, a mystery which will never be fathomed, and how some exhibit such exquisite colours is very hard to understand, though we know that the colours depend to some extent on the action of light, for bivalves, which are stationary, have rich colours on the upper valve exposed to the light, while the under valve is colourless; and, generally speaking, shells from shallow water have richer and warmer colours than those which come from deep waters, though those which inhabit the tropics are much more brilliant than those which live

in temperate regions.   But your question about the
mantle has caused me to digress considerably. As I was
telling you, there are five classes of the Mollusca; in
point of fact, there are six, but as we have nothing to do
with the sixth—*Tunicata*—inasmuch as the animals
have no shell, but only an elastic tunic, I won't bother
you with them.   The Gasteropoda is the largest class;
the Cephalopoda are the most highly organised, and
consequently the most interesting; the animals are
symmetrical—that is, they have both sides of their
bodies equally developed; they have large heads and
remarkably large eyes, and their arms or feet are
arranged in a circle round their heads; they have two
powerful jaws, not unlike the beak of a parrot; they
have a large crop, like a bird's also; the tongue is
covered with tiny horny barbed spines, and they may
be said to have three hearts, which lie between the
gills; their senses are very acute, their great eyes being
very perfect; cavities on each side of the brain serve
them as ears, but it is left for you to discover their
noses.'

'Oh! Luke, what wonderful creatures! They sound
rather terrible.'

'Terrible! I should say they were—some of them,
at least.   What will you say, Poppy, when I tell you
the dreadful Octopus is own brother to that beautiful,
delicate Argonaut which Graham is to find and send to
you? He is, indeed; at least, he belongs to the same
family.   There are six families of the Cephalopods: the
Octopoda, the Sepias, the Belemnites—they are all
fossils, so we have nothing to do with them—the

Spirulas, the Nautilidæ, and the Ammonites—which are also fossil.'

'But do you mean to say, Luke, the Argonaut is a kind of Octopus?'

'I mean to say the animal has eight arms arranged round his mouth, and is therefore included in the Octopoda. He is the beauty of the family, while his elder brother, the Octopus, is the black sheep. By the way, Poppy, the common name for the Octopus is the Cuttle-fish; they vary in size from an inch to two feet in length, while the arms of some of the largest are two feet long. These arms, or tentacles, are highly muscular and flexible, and can be twisted in any direction round any object, as well as serving as organs of motion. They are furnished with suckers on the under-surface, and if they once fix on any substance it is easier to tear the tentacle away than to release it so you may imagine what terrible enemies these large Octopi are even to man, if he comes in contact with them. Now, though in the various families these arms differ very much, yet they are all armed with these suckers. You would suppose the Octopus was sufficiently armed with these formidable suckers of his, and yet he has another method of defence common to many members of the class; he has an ink-bag, from which he discharges an inky fluid, which discolours the surrounding water, and enables him under cover of it to make good his escape from his enemies.'

'I should not think the cruel creature need be afraid of any other animal.'

'Well, the Argonaut needs it, for he is by no means

so terrible a creature as the Octopus. He uses it too if necessary, and he also uses his suckers to seize his prey, while at the same time he wraps his dilated arms round his shell, and so descends in a cloud of his own ink if alarmed. The animal of the Argonaut is very beautiful when alive; these arms and all the body are purple and silver and gold; and the great eyes of all the Cephalopods are luminous at night. I forgot to tell you that the Octopus has no shell; indeed, there are one or two species of Argonaut which have no shell also.'

'I hope there are no Octopuses in our English seas,' said Poppy, regardless of Latin grammar.

'Yes, the Octopi are found in all seas; but you need not be afraid of coming across any of the larger ones on this coast; in India and Italy the cuttle-fish is used for food. The Sepias, or Squids, as they are commonly called, are the second family; they are the literary members of the class.'

'Literary, Luke; what do you mean?'

'Well, I don't mean that they are authors exactly.'

'I should hope not,' laughed Poppy; 'as father says, there are a great many too many authors now, so we don't want any fish to take to writing.'

'Nevertheless, the Squids are furnished with a pen, and they are never seen without it. This pen, as it is called, and it is very like a pen in shape, is an inner shell. I didn't see any of them in your collection the other day, but no doubt I could find some of the Cala-maries or Loligo on the beach; they are a very common species of Sepia, used by fishermen as bait. One species, called by fishermen the Flying Squid, by naturalists *Ommastrephes*, frequently leaps out of the water like flying-fish. The Common Sepia, also called the cuttle-fish, is considered a great luxury by the Sandwich islanders. Its flesh is said to be like the meat of a lobster's claw when well cooked; its shell is used as toothpowder, ink-erasers, pumice, etcetera. Some of these Sepias grow to a very large size. They all have ten arms, armed with suckers, and sometimes with claws in addition. They have two fins, and are armed with an ink-bag, which they empty at the least sign of danger; from this fluid the pigments sepia and Indian ink are prepared. Many of the Squids are fossil, and, as I said before, all the Belemnites are, so we will pass over them and go on to the Spirulas. Do you remember seeing them ? Look, here are some : these are only three recent species.'

And as Luke spoke he took up a little box lined with pink cotton-wool, in which lay some small spiral shells, whose whorls did not touch; they were very beautiful, thin, pearly-white, and almost transparent, and of a most graceful spiral form.

'Are any of these found in England ? ' asked Poppy.

'No; but those *Peronii* have been picked up in Ireland, I believe. You won't find anything more exquisite in form than those among your shells, Poppy. Now all those four families have two gills, or *branchiæ*, and are called *Dibranchiata*, or two-gilled; the last two families have four gills, and are called *Tetrabranchiata*, from *tetra*, four, and *branchiæ*, gills. And now we come to your *Nautilus Pompilius*. I'll get him down for you

E

to hold in your hands while I talk about his family. There is only one recent genus, *Nautilus*, and only two species, *Pompilius* and *Umbilicatus*, which is very rare.'

'And is the animal which lives in this shell one of those terrible eight-armed creatures?'

'Not exactly; it has numerous tentacles—Owen says ninety—but no suckers and no ink-bladder, because its strong shell is sufficient protection. The animal is attached to the shell by two very powerful muscles; it lives in the last of its numerous chambers, which is very large. They are all connected by a siphon, or tube, which perforates them, and a flexible membrane runs through this siphuncle, lining the air-chambers. The creature is furnished with a leathery hood, which fits to the shell something like the lid of a box, and by means of it the head and tentacles can be covered up. The siphuncle enables it to rise and sink at its pleasure, for the air-chambers make it of nearly the same specific gravity as the surrounding water, and by exposing more or less of its body to the water, it rises or falls accordingly. And now, as we have run through one whole class, I think we have done enough conchology for to-day. I hope you are not tired, Poppy?'

'Oh, no! I have so enjoyed it; thank you very much, Luke. Now as a reward I'll show you *Gloria maris;* or rather you may show it to me, for my back is rather bad to-day; I daren't get up.'

'But I don't know how to open the drawer.'

'I'll tell you: father said I might, only don't tell any one else, please. The spring is in the centre or

the handle; see, if you simply take hold of the handle you might try for ever without opening it, but press against the centre of the knob and it opens at once.'

'It is very clever,' said Luke; who, before he opened the drawer, was examining two or three of the handles, which were apparently all alike.

'And so simple, almost too simple, the man said, for he thought it might be possible to open it by accident.'

'I don't think so,' said Luke, as he touched the spring and the drawer opened; but to his amazement it was empty.

'Why, Poppy, you have made a mistake; this isn't the drawer, it is empty—look.'

'Empty, Luke? It is impossible! Empty! Why, *Gloria maris* is gone! Oh, what shall I do? Gone! and there are only eleven others in the world. And in her excitement Poppy got off her sofa.

'Lie down, Poppy; please lie down; it can't be gone; don't be frightened; you have made a mistake, this isn't the drawer, there must be two secret drawers,' said Luke, trying one drawer after the other.

'But there are not; there is only that one, and *Gloria maris* was in it on Saturday evening!' exclaimed Poppy, wringing her hands and paying no heed to Luke's injunctions to lie down; when, luckily for her, the door opened, and her father and Arthur Graham walked in.

'What's up here? Poppy standing wringing her hands over her shells! Well, the sooner they are got rid of the better!' exclaimed Graham.

'Poppy, my child, lie down directly,' said Mr. Merton anxiously.

'But, father, *Gloria maris* is gone!' cried Poppy, as she suffered her father to put her back on her sofa.

'My dear child, how pale you look! Fetch her a glass of wine, Luke, please. What is it, my dear?'

'*Gloria maris*, that rarest of all my shells, the one in the secret drawer, is gone,' said Poppy.

'Nonsense! It can't be gone; no one knows how to open the drawer but you and me. Let me see. Why, yes, this is the secret drawer, and it is empty; there is no doubt about that. Some one has found out the spring besides ourselves. Perhaps they have had the grace to put the shell into one of the other drawers; let us have a search; you would know it directly, wouldn't you, Luke?'

'Oh, yes, sir; here are the other Cones, it isn't amongst them,' said Luke, as he and Mr. Merton proceeded to search every drawer, but in vain; they looked them through again and again, but there was no doubt about the matter—*Gloria maris* was gone.

'What are we to do, father?' said Poppy, turning such a little white, woe-begone face to her father, that his heart ached, not for the Glory of the Sea, but for his poor little daughter's vanished health and strength.

'You must lie still and rest, my little one, and leave me to see about this. Where are the boys? Perhaps one of them has found out the spring and dared to play some trick upon us; just see if you can find them, and send them here, Thorne, will you?'

'I will, sir,' said Graham with alacrity; for he

thought it would go hardly with the boys if they had been up to any nonsense with this wonderful shell; and he wanted to warn them, if they had, their only hope was full and immediate confession.

And certainly Mr. Merton looked rather alarming when, after a few minutes, Robert and Edward followed Graham into the drawing-room.

'Have either of you boys dared to touch any of these shells?' he demanded.

'No, father,' was the immediate response.

'Are you quite sure?'

'Certain; we don't tell lies,' said Robert indignantly.

'Mind what you are about, sir; remember you are speaking to your father, if you please.'

'I beg your pardon, father,' muttered Robert, hanging his head.

'We thought you doubted our word,' said Edward.

'No, my boys, I don't doubt you—thank God, I have never known either of you deceive me; but this is a serious affair. This was by far the most valuable of all Miss Crabbe's shells, and it has disappeared in a most extraordinary manner. I must make inquiries amongst the servants.'

'It is not at all likely that they would have touched it, is it, sir? They would not know its value,' said Thorne.

'It is not likely; but if you had asked me on Saturday night, I should have said nothing was less likely than that this drawer should have been opened and *Gloria maris* taken out within forty-eight hours. I wish your mother were back, Poppy.'

'Is Mrs. Merton away from home, then?'

'No; she is only with a sick woman, with whom she sat up all Saturday night; I think I shall leave her to question the servants when she comes in. Dear me this is a very serious business. Why, that shell is worth a fabulous sum of money—it is a fortune in itself, one might almost say.'

'I hope, sir, you will immediately communicate with the police, for it is a very unpleasant thing to have occurred,' said Thorne.

'Not more so for you than for any of us, Luke; you are one of us,' said Mr. Merton.

'Or than it is for me. How do you know I didn't break into the house on Saturday or Sunday night, and steal it?' said Arthur Graham.

'It is beyond a joke, Graham, beyond a joke; it is a profound mystery. You see, not a soul except Poppy and me knew how to open the drawer——'

'Except the man who showed us, father,' said Poppy.

'Poppy has hit it; that fellow must have got into the house on Saturday or Sunday night and stolen it,' said Robert.

'Or bribed one of the servants to steal it for him,' said Edward.

'Upon my word, loth as I am to suspect any one, I can think of no other way. I must telegraph to my solicitor at once, and ask him what I am to do,' said Mr. Merton.

Accordingly he went off at once to telegraph, leaving the young people together to discuss the matter in his absence.

CHAPTER IV.

IS STRICTLY CONCHOLOGICAL.

'And God created great whales, and every living creature that moveth, which the waters brought forth abundantly, after their kind.'—GENESIS I. 21.

'Oh! what a happy life were mine
Under the hollow-hung ocean green;
Soft are the moss-beds under the sea:
We would live merrily, merrily.'—TENNYSON.

'WELL, if any one had told me a week ago I was of less value than a shell, and that all this family would confirm that opinion, I would not have believed them, but such is the melancholy truth,' said Graham; when for a quarter of an hour after Mr. Merton had left the room, *Gloria maris* had been the sole topic of conversation.

'What do you mean, Arthur?' asked Mrs. Merton, who came in in time to catch this remark.

'Oh! mother! I am so glad you are back; my best shell, *Gloria maris*, the one that was kept in that secret drawer, has been stolen!' exclaimed Poppy; and then the story of the missing shell was told again by half a dozen voices.

'Yes,' said Graham, when the excitement had somewhat subsided, 'the Glory of the Sea is gone, and the glory of Highcliff is going to sea.'

'What do you mean by the glory of Highcliff?'

'I mean myself, of course. I flattered myself my news would cause some little excitement, not unmixed with a pang or two of regret here; but I was mistaken. I ought to have remembered that nobody is missed in this world. We miss things, even such useless things as shells, but we don't miss people. My departure is entirely swallowed up in the still greater news that Poppy's *Gloria maris*, which she first set eyes on on Saturday afternoon, has departed,' said Graham, half in fun, though there was a tone of bitterness in his voice.

'You are going away, Arthur? Why didn't you tell us before?' said Poppy regretfully.

'How could I, when you were all so full of *Gloria maris?* Yes, I am ordered to join my ship this day week, and we are off to the West Indies. I shall be able to get you plenty of shells there, Poppy, so I dare say you won't regret my departure.'

'I am very sorry you are going,' said Poppy simply, ignoring the implied reproach of Graham's remark.

'So am I. Why, Graham, losing you is a thousand times worse than losing that old shell of Poppy's,' said Edward.

'I should think it was, indeed; only, you see, Graham will come back again in five years, and *Gloria maris*, I believe, is gone for good,' said Robert.

And, though Poppy was genuinely sorry that Arthur was going, yet he could not hide from himself the

apparent truth that her regret for his departure was
swallowed up by her dismay at the mysterious disappearance of *Gloria maris;* while both Luke and Mr.
Merton were at little pains to conceal their opinion
that the loss of so valuable a shell was by far the
greater calamity, if indeed Graham's being ordered to
sea could be called a calamity. Mr. Merton received
an answer to his telegram that same evening; it was
very brief, but it left no doubt as to what he was to do,
for it said:

'Dobson will arrive by the first train to-morrow; do
nothing till he comes.'

Who Mr. Dobson was Mr. Merton had not the
remotest idea, and he awaited his arrival with no little
curiosity, going to meet him the following morning.
Mr. Dobson turned out to be a little dapper man, clean
shaven, and dressed in a blue serge suit, as the most
appropriate costume for a few days' visit at the seaside
solely for the benefit of his health. On arriving, he
plunged into business at once, and before he reached
the Rectory had taken down full particulars of the case.
He was very careful to inquire who was present when
the shells were unpacked, and who slept in the house
on Saturday and Sunday nights. He asked very few
questions about the servants, but he was particular in
his inquiries about Luke Thorne and Arthur Graham.

'Was there any talk of selling these shells?'

'Oh, dear, yes! a great deal. My daughter was most
anxious to sell them until she saw them, and Mr.
Graham was to have negotiated the matter for her
with Mr. Thorne.'

'Both those gentlemen were then in favour of selling the shells?'

'No, Mr. Thorne was strongly opposed to it; Mr. Graham was anxious to sell them. But I hope you don't for one moment suspect either of these gentlemen, Mr. Dobson? I am as sure of their innocence as I am of my own.'

'That may be, sir; but I am a detective officer, sent here to sift this matter to the bottom, and it is my duty to follow up every clue, no matter how slight. As far as I can see at present, there are only three people who could possibly have taken it : the man who brought the shells down—and he must either have broken into the house or corrupted one of the servants—or one of those gentlemen. Of course it is possible one of your own sons may have taken it and hidden it up for a lark; if so, I shall soon find that out; and before I have been many hours in the house I shall know whether there has been any collusion among the servants. It would be as well if you could pass me off as an old friend, a partner of your solicitor's; there is no harm in their knowing I have come down about the shell, but you had better keep to yourself that I am a detective. I shall have to ask you to give me a bed for a night or two, perhaps for several; and if we start as old friends my work will be done all the quicker. As you are certain of the innocence of these gentlemen, you will not feel that you are luring them on to detection by furthering my work. If you will give me the run of the house, and induce them to regard me as a friend, I think I shall very soon get to the bottom of this affair.'

Mr. Merton didn't altogether like this scheme. He could not pass a stranger off as a friend, but as he had not the very slightest doubt of the innocence of Graham and Thorne, he consented to introduce the detective to his wife as a friend of his lawyer, Mr. Seaman.

Mr. Dobson very soon made himself at home. He began by asking for a holiday for the two boys, and spent the morning with them in going over the house and premises. He casually informed them that he would give a hundred pounds to either of them if they succeeded in finding *Gloria maris*, and he came to the conclusion before they went in to dinner that neither of them had anything to do with the lost shell. At dinner he made Luke Thorne's acquaintance, and apparently took a fancy to him, for he proposed they should go for a walk together that afternoon, to which Luke agreed; only stipulating that he should be back in time to give Poppy her lesson in shells.

'Certainly; and if you'll allow me, I should like to be present and take a peep at some of these wonderful shells,' said Mr. Dobson; who before he started took occasion to give Mr. Merton a hint that he should like to see Arthur Graham that day, if it could be managed.

Mr. Dobson soon found he should have no difficulty in discussing his business with Luke Thorne, for he could talk of little else but the missing shell; but by dint of a little ingenuity he succeeded in finding out Graham and Thorne were rivals, and that the latter was by no means sorry that Graham's ship was to sail on the following Monday.

'Do you suppose Mr. Graham had any hand in this

Gloria maris affair?   Is he fond of playing tricks?
Would he have hidden it for a joke?'

'Oh, no! Graham had no more to do with it than I
had; besides, he had no opportunity.'

'Was he at church on Sunday morning?'

'No, he wasn't, now I come to remember; but I am
positive he has not touched the shell.'

Mr. Dobson was by no means so positive. He had
already found out no one was at home on Sunday
morning except the cook, and he had also discovered
that the hall door was never locked except at night.
What was there to have hindered this Mr. Graham, who
was so suddenly ordered off to sea, from walking in and
carrying off the shell while the family were at church?
By the time Mr. Dobson returned from his walk, he
felt almost as convinced of Graham's guilt as he did of
Thorne's innocence; though when, on entering the
drawing-room, he was introduced to the young sailor,
he was forced to confess he did not look like a thief.

'He may have done it for a lark,' thought the
detective, for he was not one to give up a theory he had
invented because a man looked incapable of crime.

'Here you are, Luke, we are all waiting for you.
Arthur wants to hear your lesson to me to-day, and
Mr. Dobson can be looking through the cabinets while
you are giving it me,' said Poppy, when Luke and
Mr. Dobson came in to the group before the fire.

'Let him have a cup of tea after his walk first,
Poppy,' said Mrs. Merton.

'Well, Poppy, we are to begin on the second class,
Gasteropoda, to-day; it is the largest division of the

Mollusca; it contains four orders according to the present system—Cuvier made eight—and fifty-three families, but we shall not have to deal with all those families, for some are land shells. Some few live in fresh water, and with both these we have nothing to do. The Gasteropoda may be taken as the type of the Mollusca, and the common snail as the type of the Gasteropoda.'

'What do you mean by being the type of the Mollusca?'

'I mean that they are the most characteristic of the Mollusca. On the one hand, they are less like fishes than the Cephalopoda; and, on the other hand, they are less like Zoophytes than the bivalves. They move, like the common snail, on a fleshy muscular foot, by means of which they crawl on land or on the surface of the water, for their swimming is little more than this. Very few of them can really swim or float like *Ianthina*, that pretty little violet sea-snail; some, like *Patella*, never move at all, but actually eat a hollow in the rock with this fleshy foot; some adhere to floating sea-weed. They all have a visible head, which is usually adorned with from two to six feelers; their eyes are small, and are sometimes fixed in the head, sometimes in the feelers, sometimes on separate branches. On the back is a mantle, and in most species this produces a shell; but in some few it is wanting altogether, and in some it is only rudimental. The shell is univalve and spiral usually; in one genus, *Chiton*, however, it is multivalve, and in some it is conical. Most of the spiral shells are dextral or right-handed, though exceptions sometimes occur, and a large price used to be paid formerly for a left-handed shell—I mean for a left-handed dextral, if you'll excuse the bull. Some shells, like *Clausilia*, are always sinistral or left-handed. The Gasteropoda divide themselves naturally into two orders, the water-breathers, or Branchifera, and the air-breathers, or Pulmonifera.'

'But, Luke, you told me there were four orders. If the Gasteropoda were kind enough to divide themselves into two orders, why did conchologists want to go and puzzle people by making those two into four?'

'Because they thought it easier in the end to subdivide the Branchifera into three orders: the Prosobranchiata, in which the gills are situated in advance of the heart, from the Greek *proson*; the Opistho-branchiata—'

'Oh! Luke, what a dreadful word; must I learn it?'

'I think so; *opisthen* is the Greek for rear, and the order is so called because the gills are placed in the hind part of the body; and, lastly, the Nucleobranchiata, in which the gills and digestive organs form a nucleus on the back of the animal; this last is a very small order, containing only a few families, all of which are pelagic.'

'What is pelagic, please?' asked Poppy.

'Belonging to deep seas. All these animals are found swimming on the surface of deep seas, and are therefore called pelagic. With the exception of the genus Chiton, all the shells of the Gasteropoda are formed of one single piece; Chiton is very curious, as we shall see presently, and is made of eight pieces. The shell is generally large enough to contain the animal, which coils itself up spirally, and can withdraw entirely into its house; closing the door, in many cases, with a second piece of horny shell adhering to its foot, and called the operculum. In the Gasteropods the shell is seldom internal—that is, entirely covered by the mantle, as in the Squids. No Gasteropod has a series of chambers in his house, like the Nautilus; his shell never contains more than one conical or spiral chamber, though in some spiral shells the whorls are almost separate, as in the Precious Wentle Trap (*Scalaria pretiosa*). The axis round which the whorls are coiled is sometimes hollow, and then the shell is called umbricated, or perforated; the last turn of the shell is called the body-whorl, and is usually very large; the point of the shell is called the apex, the opposite end the base. By glancing at the aperture of a shell, you can tell whether the animal was carnivorous or herbivorous; in vegetable-feeders the aperture is entire; where the animal is carnivorous it is notched, and sometimes prolonged into a canal. See, here in this *Voluta*, how deeply notched the aperture is: the animal, we may be sure, was carnivorous; or take a Cowry—see, the aperture here is channelled at both ends; these, again, are carnivorous.'

'Why, what flesh can they get to eat?' asked Poppy.

'Other molluscs, of course. Fish is flesh in this sense. There is another bull for you, Poppy; the Irish blood of my mother is in the ascendant to-day. The outer side—the right side, that is—of the aperture, is called the outer

F

lip, and in immature shells it is generally thin and sharp; in adults thickened, sometimes curled outwards, when it is called reflected; sometimes, as in the Cowry (*Cypræa*), inwards, when it is said to be inflected; and sometimes it is fringed with spines, as in *Murex*. The inner lip is called the columellar lip.'

While Luke was speaking, he took up shell after shell from time to time, and illustrated his meaning by touching the part he referred to. Mr. Dobson was in the meantime carefully examining all the cabinets, having casually asked Graham to show him the spring of the secret drawer; but Graham referred him to Mr. Merton, professing his ignorance as to how it worked.

'But now, Poppy, we must get on to the family of the Prosobranchiata. First come the Carnivorous Gasteropods, and of these the *Strombidæ*, or Wing shells, are the first family; see how deeply notched the lip is in *Strombus*. These animals are very active, as molluscs go; they feed on carrion, and they are celebrated for their large eyes, which are more perfect than any of the other Gasteropods; the foot is narrow, and so little adapted for creeping, that the animal prefers to get along by turning its shell from side to side, and thus executing a series of leaps. There are four genera: *Strombus*, which means a stromb: these are found on reefs at low water in the West Indies, Pacific, Red Sea, Indian Ocean, and Mediterranean; there are sixty species, eight of which are fossil, and one, *Strombus gigas*, as you remember, is the Fountain shell, one of the largest living shells. Then comes the genus *Pteroceras*, or

Scorpion shells, from *pteron*, a wing, and *ceras*, a horn; there are only ten living species; you have one, *lambis*, and a lovely shell it is. Look!—they come from India and China, and there are nearly a hundred fossil species. A very different-looking shell is *Rostellaria curta*, so called because the canal is prolonged like the bill of a bird, hence the name of the genus, from *rostellum*, a little beak; this shell has what we call an elongated spire. There are only five living species, all foreign, but seventy fossil, some of which are found in our chalk. The last genus rejoices in the name of Seraphs; the Latin name is *Terebellum*. There is only one species, a thin, delicate, oblong shell, marked with bands and spots; it comes from the Indian seas, and is found in a fossil state also.'

'Is that the end of the Strombidæ?'

'Yes. Now we come to the *Muricidæ*, which contain some very favourite shells.'

'My friends the Sting Winkles included,' said Robert.

'They belong to the first genus, *Murex*. The Murices are ornamented with three or more rows of varices, that is, fringes on the outer lip, which make them perhaps the most beautiful in form of all shells. *Tenuispina*, or Venus' comb, is one of the most curious; in that the varices become long spines; it is thought the Murex only makes one-third of a whorl annually, ending it in a varix. They are found all over the world, but we have only two British species, *Erinaceus*, the Sting Winkle of Robert, and *Corallinus*, the animal of which is a brilliant scarlet colour. In some species—as in *Murex*

F 2

Palma Rosa—the varices are developed into beautiful leaf-like fronds; the colours in the aperture of the genus are always very bright and of great purity of tint. Very frequently the aperture is tinged with an exquisite pink or deep rose colour, and the enamelling of the lining is very fine and profuse. The Tritons, or Conch shells, are a genus of Muricidæ——'

'But you have not told me what the animal of Murex is like. Is he as beautiful as his shell?'

'Not in colour; he has a broad flat head, with two tentacles, in the centre of which are fixed the eyes; the foot is oval, and rather small; the tongue is armed profusely with teeth, and the mantle is produced into a siphon. The animal of Triton is nearly always brilliantly coloured; it has a smaller and thicker foot than Murex, a large head, eyes in the centre of its tentacles, and a long, cylindrical proboscis, which can be projected from the mouth; Murex has a similar appendage. The shell of Triton is oblong, the varices are disconnected and placed alternately on each whorl, and are never developed into leaves or spines; the canal is prominent, the lips toothed, the outer often wrinkled, the inner sometimes thickened; the epidermis—that is, the outer skin of the shell, is thick and hairy, and sometimes tufted with bristles.'

'Have all shells an epidermis?' asked Poppy.

'Yes; sometimes it is thin and transparent, sometimes silky or fringed with hairs, sometimes thick and rough, like coarse cloth; in all fresh-water shells it is olive-coloured and thick. The colours of land-shells depend greatly on the epidermis. In the Cowry, and some other shells, it is more or less covered up by another layer of shell; in the bivalves it is connected with the mantle by organic matter.'

'What is the use of this epidermis?' said Poppy.

'It protects the shell from heat and cold and chemical agents. Some fresh-water shells would be entirely dissolved by the quantity of carbonic acid gas contained in all fresh waters, more or less, if it were not for the epidermis. It soon fades after the death of the animal; it has life, but not sensation, like our epidermis or scarf-skin. But to return to the Tritons. There are 102 species. One minute species has been found by dredging at a depth of fifty fathoms, but they are generally found at a depth ranging from low water to ten or twenty fathoms. They are found in the West Indies, the Pacific, Mediterranean, Indian Ocean, Africa, and West America; there are forty-five fossil species, some British. There is a genus called *Ranella*, or Frog shell, in which the animal is like that of Triton. The shell has two rows of varices, one on each side, united longitudinally. Some of the species are very handsome shells, all foreign. The animal of Murex is so like that of the next genus I want to talk about that they are indistinguishable—the Top shells, or *Turbinella*. They are large, heavy, and shaped like a top, or rather like a pear; the left or columellar lip has three or four folds or plaits crossing it; the shell is thick, and the operculum like a claw. One species found in Ceylon—you have one, Poppy, *Turbinella pyrum*—is called the Shank shell, and is often beautifully carved by the natives. Dextral or reversed varieties are considered sacred, and used by the priests to administer medicine. Some species are very heavy.'

'I thought these pear-shaped shells were called Pyrula,' said Robert.

'That is another genus. *Pyrula* is shaped like a pear or a fig; hence the name, from *pyrus*, a pear. The animal of Pyrula has a long, narrow head with two small tentacula, at the base of which are the eyes; the foot is moderately large. In one species, *Pyrula ficus*, the mantle forms lobes on the sides, which nearly meet over the back of the shell. Another very rare species, *rapa*, has the spire quite flat, so that it will stand upright if placed on the spire. Some species are found in the Northern Ocean, but the greater number are tropical.'

'There don't seem to be any British shells worth mentioning, Luke,' grumbled Edward.

'That is only because he is going straight through Poppy's collection,' said Robert.

'Indeed I am not; I am going straight through the families just as they come; there is no particular order for the genera. However, I'll take *Fusus*, or the Spindle shells, next. There are six British species; the shell is a graceful shape, like a spindle; the canal and spire both frequently very long; the left lip is smooth, the right toothed or waved. They are not at all brilliantly coloured, but owe their beauty to their form. The animal has a large oval foot, thick tentacles flanking the head and bearing the eyes, a long proboscis, and the tongue armed with teeth. One British species, *Fusus antiquus,* is called the Red Whelk, and is eaten largely in Scotland, where it also goes by the name of the 'Buckie,' or the 'Roaring Buckie,' because the sound of the sea may always be heard in it. One species found off Spitzbergen is always reversed, and is called *Fusus deformis*. *F. colosseus* is often eleven inches long, and is one of the two largest living Gasteropods. *F. longissimus* is very long and turreted. The animal of Fusus and another genus, *Fasciolaria*, are exactly alike. One species, *Fasciolaria gigantea*, grows to two feet long in the Southern seas; they are natives of the Indian Ocean. There are sixteen living species, but they are not numerous animals; the colours are rather brighter than Fusus; the shell fusiform, but with a shorter spine and canal than the Spindles. Some species are found in the Mediterranean.'

'How many more genera are there in that family, Luke? for it is getting rather late,' said Mr. Merton.

'Only three, sir; I will run through them very quickly. The first, *Pisania*, often confounded with *Buccinum* and *Murex*; the shell has numerous indistinct varices; it is very numerous, there are 120 species, mostly found on the shores of Africa, India, and America. The second, *Cancellaria*, is a vegetable-feeding genus; see, Poppy, here is a specimen, no notch in the aperture, though channelled in front. The shell is cancellated, that is, cross-barred, hence the name. The columella has several strongly marked folds; the foot of the animal is almost as long as the shell, but very thin; the head is broad and flat; the tentacles long and slender, bearing the eyes at the base.'

'This is Cancellaria, this striped shell: how rough it feels!' said Graham.

'Yes, they are generally rough. They are rare, but not very handsome; there are seventy living species; some fossil species are British. Now we come to the last genus, *Trichotropis*, from *thrix*, hair; and *tropis*, keel.'

'What a dreadful name! and it is sure to be tropical,' grumbled Robert.

'No, it is not, it is British; at least one species, *Borealis*, and that the typical species, is found on our coasts. The shell is thin, spiral, and furrowed; the ridges of the epidermis fringed; the animal has a short, broad head, the tentacles wide apart, with the eyes in the middle, and a long proboscis. There are eight species, all found in Northern seas, and with Trichotropis I will finish for to-day.'

Poppy thanked Luke for his lesson, and the others joined her, all professing to have been very much interested in it, except the two little boys, and they were quite aggrieved that the British shells had been scarcely alluded to; they seemed to regard it as little short of a personal insult.

'Well, suppose I make my lecture exclusively on British shells, merely exhibiting a few of Poppy's foreign shells, to show them how the species vary under the influence of climate; how would that be, sir?' said Thorne, turning to Mr. Merton. But the boys were so enthusiastic in their approbation, that at first their father could not edge in a word.

'I think it would do very well; it may fire some of our villagers with a desire to search our rocks for specimens,' said Mr. Merton.

'I wish you could have your lecture before I start,' said Graham.

'I could, I dare say, if Mr. Merton does not object to its being on Saturday evening; I can't be ready before, i it is to be on British shells.'

'Saturday is a bad night,' objected Mr. Merton.

'I am sorry for that, for I should very much like to be present at this lecture. If you could put me up till Monday, I could just get down in time on Saturday evening; I am due in London to-morrow,' said Mr. Dobson, with a significant glance at Mr. Merton; who, seeing the detective desired the lecture to take place on the Saturday, for some reason best known to himself, at once removed his objections, and the matter was settled. The truth was, Mr. Dobson was at present fairly baffled, though he would not have confessed it, even to himself. His suspicions rested on Graham, but he had not at present a jot of evidence against him, beyond the mere facts that he saw the shells unpacked, knew the value of *Gloria maris*, and had the opportunity, supposing that he had mastered the spring of the secret drawer, of getting possession of the treasure on Sunday morning, when every one else was at church. But all this was mere suspicion, there was absolutely no case against him; and Mr. Dobson was well aware he must get hold of some more tangible evidence than this, if he wished to prevent his prey from sailing the following Monday. There was a whole week for him to act in, and, as he knew, a great deal could be done in a week. Meanwhile, it was his duty to inquire into the character of the packer; and for that purpose, among others, he was going to London the next day. There, too, he would set afloat inquiries as to whether any *Gloria maris* had been offered for sale during the last few days; he would be certain to hear of it from the London conchologists, if so invaluable a species had been in the market. He did not in the least suspect the packer, for he felt certain no burglary had been committed, and none of the Rectory servants had wit enough, in his opinion, to have had any hand in the business; they could not even realise the fact that the shells were valuable. So Mr. Dobson spent the following day in roaming about the village, trying to elicit information from the villagers as to Mr. Arthur Graham's movements on Sunday morning; but only arriving at the news that he had been seen to go down to the beach with his dogs, while the people were in church. No one remembered seeing him in the neighbourhood of the Rectory, and the detective went to London, feeling this was a tougher job than he had anticipated.

The Edible Snail

CHAPTER V.

THE LECTURE.

'Thou art worthy, O Lord, to receive glory and honour and power : for Thou hast created all things, and for Thy pleasure they are and were created.'—REVELATION IV. 11.

'Forthwith the sounds and seas, each creek and bay
  With fry innumerable swarm, and shoals
  Of fish that with their fins and shining scales
  Glide under the green wave, in sculls that oft
  Bank the mid-sea, part single or with mate
  Graze, the sea-weed their pasture, and through groves
  Of coral stray, or sporting with quick glance
  Show to the sun their waved coats dropt with gold,
  Or in their pearly shells at ease attend
  Moist nutriment, or under rocks their food,
  In jointed armour watch.'—MILTON.

IF Mr. Dobson went up to London feeling puzzled on the Tuesday, he returned to Highcliff on the Saturday no wiser, but more firmly convinced than ever that Graham must be the culprit, though he had no hope of bringing the crime home to him. He had learnt that the packer was a thoroughly honest, trustworthy man, and, moreover, would have no difficulty in proving that he was in London on the Saturday evening, and had been there ever since, so that it was quite impossible he had anything to do with it.

'No,' said Mr. Dobson to himself; 'it is the young squire; and if it ain't him it is the pupil, though I have not a jot of evidence against either, and, as far as looks go, one is as innocent as the other; it strikes me this business will prove too much for me after all, if I don't look sharp; and sharp I mean to look to-night at this lecture, I can tell them.'

He made his way straight from the station to the school-room in which the lecture was to take place. The room was well filled, and Luke Thorne was on the platform with a table set out with shells in front of him, just about to begin his lecture when Mr. Dobson entered. A place had been reserved for him near the Rectory party, but he did not avail himself of it, and took up a standing position near the platform, from which he could command a good view, not only of the lecturer but of the audience; and there he stood the greater part of the evening, apparently carelessly looking about him and listening to the lecture, though it is doubtful if he heard a word of it, so absorbed was he in his own thoughts.

It is not our intention to do more than summarise the lecture, because to report it *verbatim* would be to repeat a great deal that has been already said; for

Luke first of all described the organisation and classification of the Mollusca, in as simple language as he
could find.

'Molluscs, my friends, are creatures with a soft body
protected by an external shell, and in the animal
kingdom they come between fishes and the Articulata;
in other words, they rank below salmon, cod, herring,
&c., which are vertebrate animals, and above crabs and
lobsters, which, strictly speaking, have no shell, but
only a hard covering. The oyster, the mussel, and
the garden snail are types of the Molluscs, but I
am going to confine my lecture to-night to Marine
Molluscs, that is, those which inhabit the sea; moreover,
I am only going, by express desire, to speak of those
Molluscs which inhabit our own British seas. Now,
as perhaps some of you know, Molluscs produce their
young from eggs, and the eggs of sea shells adhere
together in masses. They are most prolific animals;
for instance, mussels and oysters are said to produce
between 200,000 and 300,000 young in one season.
The bivalves and the tunicaries are hatched before they
leave their parent, and many of the former—like the
cockle and mussel—attain their full growth in a year,
but the oyster goes on enlarging his shell for four or
five years.

'The Molluscs are as clever as birds and butterflies in
placing their eggs where they will be safe from injury,
and near the proper food for the young when hatched.
In their infancy the different families are very much
alike, though they grow up as widely different as the
oyster and the octopus; and the fry are as different from

their parents as caterpillars from butterflies, or nearly so. In their extreme youth they all swim, and often travel to great distances; whereas many of the full-grown Molluscs, like the oyster, never move at all. Others creep on the shore or the surface of the sea, a few float, fewer really swim. The sedentary species soon tire of these wanderings; and after a few days cruising about settle down on the spot they intend to occupy for the rest of their lives. The Molluscs are great eaters, and are largely eaten themselves; not only by man but by other animals, as the rat, the otter, the racoon, the whale, and sea-birds, but their greatest enemies of all are themselves, for they prey largely on each other. Scarcely half of them are vegetable feeders, the sea-pastures of sea-weed afford no attraction to the larger half of the Marine Molluscs; they prefer flesh-meat, and prey on other shell-fish, or on zoophytes. Some like living fish, others prefer dead and putrid remains. All the bivalves feed on Infusoria, that is, microscopic insects, and on microscopic vegetables, which are brought to them by currents they have the means of exciting. Every species has its own special situation, where it finds its favourite food, and is best preserved from the dangers most liable to its kind. Every zone of sea-depth has its appropriate Molluscs; on sandy flats we find the cockle flourishing; on muddy shores the mussel; between low and high water marks the periwinkle, which loves to be left dry twice a day; the Top shells among the sea-weed at low tide; in water four or five fathoms deep, the Oyster; in deeper water the Scallop; in deepest of all the Lamp shells; in the open

sea, far from sight of land, the Sea Snails, and thousands
of other Molluscs floating on the surface of the waters.

'Now, as I wish this lecture to be useful as well as
instructive, I propose to speak to you first of those British
Molluscs which are good for food; and I suppose we
shall all agree that the best of these is the oyster; which
even in the days of ancient Greece and Rome was
considered a great delicacy. It is one of the most
sedentary of all the Molluscs, and spends its life
fixed on a rock or some other object, where its only
movement is opening and shutting its valves. It is
attached by its under-valve to its resting-place, and
at its birth is covered with a mucilaginous or slimy
liquid which causes it to stick to any object on which
it is placed. In some American and Indian rivers
oysters are found adhering to the trunks of trees, and
are called tree-oysters; they are excellent food. The
greatest enemy of the oyster is a sponge, which eats
small round holes into the valves, until the shell
is quite destroyed and falls to pieces. The shell
of the oyster is unequal; the upper valve is flat or
concave, the other convex, often plaited or foliated
and beaked; the interior is slightly nacreous. The
shells become very thick with age. The animal is shaped
like the shell; the mantle is doubly fringed; the valves
are attached by a strong round muscle, which forms
the gristle, considered by some epicures as the best
part of the oyster.

'Belonging to the same family as the oyster is the
Pecten, or Scallop, two species of which, the Scallop and
the Quin, are considered delicacies. There are nine

British species of Pecten, they are all very pretty shells; the edible Pecten is called *Pecten maximus*; the shell is regular, eared, nearly round and ribbed or furrowed; the hinge margins are straight, united by a narrow ligament. The animal is bright orange or scarlet, with a row of round black eyes at the base; the gills are remarkably delicate, the foot is shaped like a finger. Most of the Pectens spin a byssus, or threads, when young. Unlike the stay-at-home oyster, they have the power of moving rapidly through the water by suddenly contracting their muscles. The heart-shaped shell of the cockle has given it its Latin name of *Cardium*, from a Greek word *kardia*, which means the heart. The shell is so common I need not describe it. As you all know, it is equi-valve, the borders of the valves toothed and locking into each other. The animal has a very large foot, sickle-shaped; the margins of the mantle are plaited. There are two hundred species; it is found in all parts of the globe buried in the sand near the shore. Some foreign species are very pretty.

'The Sea Mussel, *Mytilus*, is at some seasons poisonous, though the cause is unknown; nevertheless thousands are eaten annually, particularly in Scotland, and tens of thousands are used for bait. Mussels produce inferior pearls, and are collected for the sake of them; they are of world-wide distribution, and have a great propensity to hide themselves by burrowing and even by spinning a nest of sand; they attach themselves by a byssus, spun from their long slender foot. There is quite a trade carried on in some parts of the country in the seed pearls found in the mussel; these are collected and sold for about two shillings an ounce. The shells when polished are of a beautiful purple colour.

'In Jersey and Guernsey a very favourite fish is the Ormer, or *Haliotis*, which is found in abundance round the Channel Islands. The shell is ear-shaped—hence its name of the Sea Ear—and perforated by a series of holes. When polished it is used largely for ornamental purposes. The animal has a very large round foot, with which it adheres firmly to the rocks like a limpet. A less well-known edible Mollusc is the Solen, or Razor Fish, which is said to be the most delicious of shell-fish if well cooked; it is best broiled. Most of you here know how to catch the Solen better than I do; but perhaps you don't know that the animal has a large powerful foot, which enables it to bury itself as it does in the sand.

'The Whelk, or *Buccinum*, called also the Trumpet shell, is much eaten in the North of England, where it is dredged and also used as bait. There are four British species, but the genus is known all over the world. The shells have no bright colours, but they vary very much in shape and sculpture; they are generally oval, with a large body-whorl and a spire of round whorls. Sometimes the shells are small and very thick, sometimes large and thin. The animal has a large flabby foot, and eyes at the base of its tentacles. The Red Whelk, or "Buckie," of Scotland, is the Spindle shell or Fusus, and is much better eating than the common Whelk. Perhaps the commonest of our English Molluscs used as food is the Periwinkle, the *Littorina* of conchologists, for it is to be found crawling about

G

between watermarks on all parts of our coast; it gets
its Latin name from *litus*, the sea-shore.   There are
nine or ten British species; it abounds here and also in
Sweden, where it is used as a weather-glass by the
peasants, who say that whenever a storm is near, the
periwinkles ascend the rocks, to avoid the dashing of the
waves, but in calm weather they descend to the sand.

'The largest British bivalve, the *Pinna*, is sometimes
used for food, but it requires a great deal of cooking to
make it tender.   Our British species is seldom more
than a foot long, but foreign species grow to two feet in
length, and one foot in breadth at the broader end, for
the shell is wedge-shaped.   Some fossil species have been
found in the Cotswold Hills which must have measured
a yard across, and an inch or more in thickness; but in
our degenerate times they do not attain such gigantic
proportions.   When young the shell of the Pinna is thin,
brittle, and translucent, with a thin pearly lining.   The
animal is triangular, the mantle doubly fringed, the gills
long, the foot rather small; from it the creature spins a
powerful byssus, which is attached to the centre of each
valve by large muscles, and by it the Pinna is generally
found moored to the sand, the beak plunged deep into
the ground, the other end, which is always gaping,
turned upwards.   Small amber-coloured pearls of little
value are sometimes found within the shell, and a tiny
crab often takes up its abode under shelter of the
Pinna's mantle, where apparently it is a welcome guest,
perhaps because it can see, whereas the Pinna is blind.
At any rate, many tales are told of this strange friend-
ship, and Aristotle gave the crab the name of the

Pinna's guardian. In Italy and Sicily the creature is sought as an article of food, and also for the sake of its long, silky, shining byssus, from which a soft warm species of cloth is made, but which, strange to say, will not take any dye. In the Natural History Museum is a pair of gloves spun from this byssus, and Pope Benedict XV. once had a pair of stockings made from it.

'In North America and Zetland the *Mya arcnaria,* or Gaper, as we call it, is considered an excellent dish, but I am not aware that it is eaten in England, though this very species is common on our own coasts. It is found in the deep sea and also on the beach near high water-mark; it burrows a foot deep in the sand, leaving a hole which betrays its place of retreat. In Greenland it is preyed upon by the walrus, the Arctic fox, and birds. The shell is thick, strong, and opaque, covered with a wrinkled epidermis. It is bivalve, oblong, the left valve smaller than the right; the mantle is closed except in one place, where it opens to admit the passage of the small foot; the shape of the body is a long broad tube. The shell gapes, hence the name.

'One of the most beautiful families of shells is the *Veneridæ,* or Venuses, and most species of the genus *Venus* are eaten, if not here, in America and on the Continent; one species, *Tapes,* is a favourite food on many parts of the Continent, where it grows to a larger size than here. The shell is an oval bivalve; the animal spins a byssus from its thick foot. The *Venus mercuraria* is used by the North American Indians as money, and also as beads and ornaments for their dresses; the shells and animals of the Veneridæ vary very much, and conchologists are not agreed as to their classification. They are all remarkable for their graceful shapes and beautiful colours, and though these are more remarkable in tropical species yet we have some very pretty British species. For instance, *Cytherea* is a beautiful shell; it is large, smooth, oval, pinkish, marked with rich brown outside, white within. The animal is orange-red, with a beautifully scalloped mantle.

I must not forget to mention an edible Mollusc which is largely eaten in Ireland, particularly in seasons of scarcity—the Limpet, or *Patella*, from a Latin word meaning a dish. It is not very nice food, but when boiled makes a meal for our seaside poor when times are bad, and has often saved shipwrecked mariners from starvation; it is also largely used as bait by fishermen. We have three British species, *Patella vulgata*, the Common Limpet; *Patella athletica*, which resembles *vulgata* very closely, though if used as bait it is refused by fishes, who at once detect the difference; and *Patella pellucida*, the Transparent Limpet, a pretty little dark olive shell rayed with blue, which is semi-transparent. The genus possesses the power of adhering so firmly to rocks that the heaviest seas may break over it without washing it off. Come what may, stones, shingle, mighty waves, there sticks the Limpet, secure in its cone-shaped shell, fixed firmly on the rock to which it adheres by atmospheric pressure of fifteen pounds to the square inch.

Our common Limpet is one of the most sedentary; it seems never to move from one spot, and forms a cavity in the rock itself by absorbing some of its substance. Nevertheless the creature can move if it chooses, particularly when young, when it can crawl, and leaves a track on the rock which it scrapes. It manages to get change twice a day, for it lives between tide-marks, so it is left high and dry twice every day; it is said to be able to lift its shell and spring to some distance, but I cannot vouch for the truth of this statement. When removed from its shell, the animal will be found to have left a muscular impression in the form of a horse-shoe. It has a distinct head with tentacles and eyes at the base; the mouth is armed with horny jaws and a long ribbon-shaped toothed tongue, the foot is a large disk. Some species move occasionally, others fix themselves on sea-weeds— the food of the whole tribe of Limpets, as far as is known. In Cyprus and the Cape of Good Hope a large species abounds, the shells of which are used as spoons by the Hottentots, and in South America there is a still larger species, one foot in diameter. These shells are used as basins by the natives; we should find a difficulty in performing our ablutions in the shell of our common Limpet, which is a mere liliputian in comparison.'

Here the audience broke into a laugh, and the lecturer paused to rest for a minute, under cover of which interruption Mr. Dobson took occasion to move from his place by the platform, and by a little judicious manœuvring succeeded in seating himself between

Arthur Graham and Mr. Merton, which was precisely the position he wished to occupy.

'By the kindness of Miss Merton,' resumed the lecturer, ' I am enabled to show you a few specimens of some of the most beautiful foreign shells, the genera of which are but feebly if at all represented in our cold climate. Of the most valuable family, the Cones, we have not a single species, but I am able to show you several very handsome specimens; and I will take this opportunity of telling you, that in this little village, in the Rectory last Saturday or Sunday, a shell called the Glory of the Sea, worth a fabulous sum of money, was stolen from a cabinet; if any one here can give us any information which may lead to the recovery of this treasure, I can safely promise in the Rector's name that he or she shall be handsomely rewarded.'

Here Mr. Dobson, who was narrowly watching Arthur Graham, mentally made a note that the lecturer was innocent; and as his prey, in his own language, did not turn a hair, he began to be impressed with his innocence.

' We shall see, we shall see; I shall stay here till Monday, and then if nothing turns up my gentleman will sail, and George Dobson will have to confess himself beaten for once in his life,' reflected Mr. Dobson; while Luke went on to say that Miss Merton possessed no other shell of anything like the value of *Gloria maris*; for, as he afterwards told Poppy, he thought he had better make this clear, lest another robbery should be attempted.

' Of the Cowries, one of the handsomest shell-

families, we have only one representative, and that a
very inadequate one, for *Cypræa Europea*, or the Nun
Cowry, is a little dull-coloured shell possessing none of
the beauty of its tropical relations. It is common
enough on our coast, and no doubt many of you have
often picked up a little flesh-coloured shell, ribbed
across the back, and opening all down the under-side,
about the size of a coffee-berry, this is the Nun Cowry.
The animal is so much larger than the shell, that it is
wonderful how it manages to conceal itself so completely inside it, but it does. It is a bright orange-
colour, and about an inch and a half long. The shell is
so wrapped up in the lobes of the bright mantle as to
be almost concealed from view. The head has three
horns, on the two outer ones are fixed the eyes; the body
is convex, and the foot flat, on which the creature crawls.

'The beautiful Murexes are only feebly represented
in this country; we have two species, *Murex corallinus*,
and *Murex erinaceus*, but neither are at all characteristic of the genus either in shape or colour. *Purpura*,
a near relation of the Murexes, is represented here by
one species, *lapillus*, which is very abundant on our
coasts, as the *Trochus* and Winkle know to their cost;
for it is as greedy a creature as the beautiful Murex,
and, like that sea-tiger, feeds on living victims. The
animal resembles Murex, and is of a yellowish colour
with conspicuous eyes; the shell is spindle-shaped,
with a thick outer lip and a well-marked canal; the
whorls of the spire are turreted and ribbed. The
creature secretes a purple dye, which is quite as good
as the dye of the celebrated Murex, which furnished the

Tyrian purple, and was formerly used in Ireland; but it cannot be obtained in sufficient quantities to make it worth while to employ it now. This dye is contained in a receptacle behind the head of *Purpura;* it can be obtained by pressing on the operculum. It is a white fluid, but on being exposed to the air yields a rich purplish-crimson colour. The eggs of this animal are deposited in a membrane or egg-bag, and are commonly called the Dog Periwinkle, as many of you no doubt are aware. *Purpura* preys on limpets and periwinkles and mussels; it bores a hole through the shells of these fish, and then sucks up the juicy morsel. It will spend perhaps two days in boring through a shell, it will then gorge itself with its contents, and lie for weeks before attempting to get another meal. It is to be found on the shore between the tide-marks crawling about seeking what it may devour. A very handsome and rare British shell of the Murex family is a Spindle shell, *Fusus berniciencis*, it is about two inches and a half long, of a graceful fusiform or spindle-shaped pattern, and a delicate pink colour underneath the epidermis. A commoner species is *Fusus antiquus*, a large solid oval shell, sometimes white, beautifully tinged with orange inside the mouth, but oftener some shade of brown. You may occasionally meet with a sinistral or reversed shell of this species; it is used as a lamp in the North, the body-whorl is filled with oil, and a wick passed through the canal. Generally speaking, our British shells are very inferior in colour to foreign species, but this is not the case with the Staircase shells (*Scalaria*), which though far less elegant in form are quite as prettily coloured as their tropical brothers and sisters. We have five British species of these Wentle Traps, as they are commonly called. The shell is spiral, and many-whorled; its great peculiarity is that each whorl is crossed at regular intervals by circular bands or ridges. These were formed by the thickened lips of former mouths at regular periods, when the mantle, instead of secreting the shell in smooth layers, rolls it up into a varix or ridge. This animal also secretes a purple dye. It preys on smaller molluscs; it has a proboscis-like mouth, two long pointed tentacles placed close together, with eyes at their base, and a triangular foot with a fold in front. Our common Wentle Trap is a pale fawn colour, with white varices, both shell and ridges spotted with purple; a rarer species, *clathratula*, is small and white, with sharp varices.

'I must not forget to mention some of our British Sea Snails, for the genus *Natica* is very interesting. One curious fact about it is, the animal makes a nest in which it deposits its eggs. Perhaps some of you may have come across a thin coil of gristle coated with sand, deposited on some ledge of rock, or perhaps on the sand. This is the nest of the Natica, and contains the germs of young Naticæ glued together. Another peculiarity of the Natica is the large size of the animal compared with the small shell in which it retreats, closing the aperture firmly with the hard operculum it carries on its foot. To see it resting when left high and dry by the tide, with part of its shell hidden in the lobes of the mantle, and its great foot spread out on the sand, it would seem impossible that all that mass of flesh could ever be concealed inside the little shell. Natica is a very good swimmer, and also crawls along the sand under water on its broad foot. It is carnivorous, feeding on small bivalves, and is, in its turn, the prey of the cod and haddock; it has a toothed tongue, which assists it greatly in devouring its food; the head is long, hidden by a sort of veil in front; the eyes are either wanting or very rudimentary. We have seven British species. The pretty little *Ianthina*, or Violet Snail, may perhaps be called British, inasmuch as stress of weather often drives large numbers of them to our western coasts from their home in the mid ocean. Three species visit us. If thrown on the sand, it is quite incapable of returning to its native element; there it lies, staining the shore with its purple fluid, which, like the cuttle-fish, it has the power of ejecting as a means of defence.

'By the way, only a few species of these formidable creatures, the Cuttle-fish, or Cephalopoda, are British; we find the common Octopus among the rocks, generally hidden in the crevices, voraciously watching for some unhappy animal to come within reach of one of its cruel long arms, from the embrace of which nothing need hope to escape alive. The hideous creature sometimes entrenches itself in a small fort made of pebbles, from which, unseen itself, it can look out for food to satisfy its voracity. We also have the chameleon-like *Eledone*, which has the power of changing not only its colour but its appearance at its will; it is smaller than the Octopus. The Flying Squid, *Sepia*, *Sepiola*, and *Loligo*, are all British, but as they have no external shell I won't trouble you with them. Some of our very brightest-coloured and loveliest shells are the Tellens; but though the house is beautiful, the animal itself is generally of a dirty white colour. They are bivalves, generally closed, and the valves equal; the splendid *Tellina crassa* is indeed a brilliant shell of a rich pink colour, rayed with a patch of yellow at the base. The Setting Sun, or *Psammobia vespertina*, which lives buried in the mud or sand, is clouded inside with rich purple. *Psammobia tellinella* is a pretty little smooth oval shell, orange marked, with pink lines. We have nine species of *Tellina*, three of *Psammobia;* the former genus may be known by a fold in the hinder part of the shell; like Psammobia, *Tellina* lives buried in the sand at some distance from the shore. Scarcely less beautiful, both in form and colour, is the pear-shaped *Neœra*, a bivalve, pyriform, sometimes, as in *Cuspidata*, found in deep water off our northern coast, with a curved beak. To the same family (Myacidæ) belongs also the *Panopœa*, known among our fishermen as the " Bacca box," which it is supposed to resemble in shape. We have but one species—a solid shell, not unlike *Mya truncata*. Another beautifully-tinted shell is the *Pandora*, a very thin, flat, exquisitely nacreous bivalve, delicately tinted with rainbow hues, of which we have two species. Time does not allow me to speak to you of the Chitons, or coats of mail, those strange shells which have the power of rolling themselves up like a hedgehog, and are represented here by ten small species; nor of the pretty little Turret shells—that brown spiral tower you know so well; nor of the eccentric-shaped *Aporrhais*, our nearest approach to the *Strombus*, nor of the *Pholidæ*, or Borers; but if I have induced any of

you to search among our rocks for some of these lovely
and interesting treasures of the deep, I shall have
fulfilled my object. In conclusion, I would say that I am
sure none of you will take up the study of conchology
without feeling how infinitely surpassing all human
wisdom is the wisdom of God, who made all these
strange and wonderful creatures, and adapted each one
so perfectly to its environment. A very slight study of
their habits will suffice to convince you of this, and the
more deeply you enter into the subject, the deeper, too,
will be your appreciation—I use the word in all reverence
and humility—of the Divine wisdom, and, I trust also,
the deeper your confidence in Him who doeth all things
well ; for, remember if He condescends to think of the
welfare of the snail and the oyster, the delicate Paper
Nautilus, and the priceless *Gloria maris*, so, too, does
He think far more of the welfare of the poor and
ignorant, as well as of the refined and the rich. Well,
then, may we, with the Psalmist, call upon the seas,
and all that moveth therein, to praise Him, for truly
His ways are wonderful, and His wisdom past finding
out.'

And after a few words thanking the audience for
their attention, Luke Thorne sat down ; and the lecture
being over, the party broke up, most of the number
professing themselves quite satisfied with their evening's
entertainment. The only person who was disappointed
was Mr. Dobson, and he went back to the Rectory
oppressed with a sense of failure ; for he was now
convinced that whether Arthur Graham or Luke Thorne
had stolen *Gloria maris* or not, he had not a particle of

evidence against either of them ; therefore, all he could do was to confess he had failed to discover the thief, and return to London; with the understanding that if anything further was heard of it, he was to be communicated with at once.

CHAPTER VI.

ROBERT AND EDWARD ARE OVER-ZEALOUS.

'All things were created by Him, and for Him.'—Col. i. 16.

'We would run to and fro, and hide and seek,
On the broad sea-wolds in the crimson shells
Whose silvery spikes are nighest the sea.'—Tennyson.

Arthur Graham had been gone to sea more than two months before Luke Thorne had an opportunity of resuming his lessons with Poppy; for the lecture had taken up so much of his time that his studies with Mr. Merton had been somewhat neglected, and Mr. Merton, partly on this account, partly because he was dreadfully afraid of encouraging the shell-mania, as he called it, too much, had decreed that no more lessons in conchology were to be given for at least a month, which period, he said, Poppy would require to digest the lecture. Luke was more put out by this than he cared to acknowledge, for he quite misinterpreted the Rector's motive; he suspected the object was to prevent him from being so much with Poppy, whereas no such thought had entered her father's head; it never occurred to him that she was old enough to have a lover, and he certainly never suspected that his pupil entertained more than a brotherly regard for her.

Then Christmas came, and Luke went home to spend it with his own people, and did not return till the middle of January, when, to Poppy's delight, he told her he was prepared to renew their lessons without encroaching on any of her father's time.

'I suppose nothing more has been heard of *Gloria maris*,' he asked, as he prepared to renew his lesson.

'No, nothing; and, Luke, please don't mention it before father, it has so worried him. He has been up to London twice to see his lawyer about it since it was lost. He is much more vexed than even I am; mother says she can't understand his taking it so much to heart, and Mr. Seaman, his solicitor, seems quite as put out about it as father.'

'Well, it is such a valuable thing to lose, I don't wonder he is vexed about it; and, then, it has disappeared in such a mysterious manner. Poppy, I know you will tell me : do you think it possible he suspects either me or Graham of having taken it ?'

'I am certain he does not; and I know nothing would grieve him more than if he thought you imagined he suspected you.'

'I don't imagine it; but still he would be perfectly justified in doing so. However, we won't discuss such an unpleasant topic. Let us see, I left off with the second family of the Gasteropoda; to-day we begin with the *Buccinidæ*. It is a very interesting family, and includes among others the Whelks, the Harp shells, the

Dog Whelks, Purpura, the Helmet shells, Dolium, the
Olives, the Auger shells, the Ivory shells, and about
twelve other less known genera. Now, the *Buccinum*,
or Whelk, gives its name to the family; the principal
family characteristics are, the animals are similar to
Murex; they are carnivorous, the shells consequently
notched in front, or else the canal is produced into a
kind of varix on the front of the shell. I described
the Whelk and Purpura in my lecture, so I need only
say you may sometimes find a round mass resembling
coralline on the beach; this is the young fry of the
Whelk, contained in capsules which are conglomerated,
perhaps on an oyster shell, into one of these balls, and
thrown ashore. The Dog Whelk, or *Nassa*, is common
enough on our coasts at low water; the shell is like
Buccinum, but the animal, besides having a broad foot
with horns in front, has two funny little tails behind.
The Harps are beautifully shaped shells; and *Harpa
ventricosa*, the commonest, is also one of the most
beautiful; *Imperialis* is very rare indeed, and formerly
fetched an enormous price. The ridges which make the
harp-like strings are very close together in this species,
which is also beautifully coloured and marked. They
are found in the Mauritius, where there is a fishery for
them; they are taken at night when they are feeding.'

'Are these ribs former mouths?' asked Poppy,
handling some Harps as she spoke.

'Yes, undoubtedly they are; the animal has a very
large crescent-shaped foot, and when irritated it is said
to be able to drop a piece of this foot and retire completely inside its shell. There are only nine species,

none British. This large, light, globular shell, with a small spire and a very large mouth, is one of the *Dolii; Dolium,* by the way, means a tun. One species, *galea,* is found in the Mediterranean; but as a rule they come from the Indies, Africa, and South America, and are sometimes found as large as a man's head on reefs, but they are always remarkably thin and fragile. The animal, which is often of brilliant colours—blue, green, and various other shades—is very voracious, and at the same time very lazy, in its habits. It has a very large and very elastic foot, which can be spread out to an enormous size by sucking up a quantity of water. The Helmet shells, or *Cassis,* I think I described to you some time ago. The animal, which sometimes grows to an enormous size, as does the shell, has a large head, ending in a sort of snout, with two tentacula, bearing the eyes at their base. The foot is a large, thin, flat disk, and the mantle is very peculiar; it makes a sort of veil over the head, and is also prolonged into a reflected breathing-tube. The Olives are a large genus, and very common, though many of the shells are very pretty; and by filing them they can be made into variously-coloured shells. They are naturally polished, for the foot of the animal, which is very large, half covers the shell and keeps it bright. The mantle lobes are large, and these also meet over the back of the shell; the foot has no operculum. The animals are very active; they bury themselves in the sand as the tide falls, and if placed on their backs can turn over. They are fished for with lines baited with other fish. The *Terebra,* or Auger shells, are sometimes called

H

Needle shells, from their long, slender, spiral shape ; they are turreted, but distinguished from *Turritella*, which they are very like, by their notched mouth. Some species are ten inches in length. Very few are European. There are 109 species, but most of these are tropical. The animal is blind, or sometimes has tiny eyes placed on some minute tentacles. These creatures sometimes creep out of the water, but they never go beyond reach of the spray. I believe you have *Terebra pretiosa*, Poppy ? '

'Yes, I know I have; see how exquisitely it is marked, and how gracefully the whorls are curved.'

'You have not *maculata*, though; if Graham goes to Ceylon, he might send you one. Now for *Eburna*, or the Ivory shells. They are pure white, spotted with dark red, smooth and solid, and generally found minus their epidermis ; they are found in Australia and in the Indian and Chinese seas. The animal is spotted, like the shell. And now, if it is not too much for our feelings, we will go on to the Cones. They all have this much in common : the shell is inversely conical, the mouth long and narrow, the outer lip notched, and the operculum very small. The animal has a snout-like head, with eyes on the tentacles ; the tentacles themselves are far apart ; the foot is oblong, the tongue armed with prickles.'

'I should not care to handle them if the animal were alive, with a prickly tongue and a tendency to bite.'

'I think only one species, *Anticus*, bites; they all prey on other sea-animals, though, and if you wanted to catch one you would have to handle it, for they are generally found in holes of rocks or coral reefs. They are all tropical, except a few species which inhabit the Mediterranean.'

'Are they all very rare?'

'Oh, no; but many species are, like *Gloria maris*, *Cedo nulli*, Field of the Cloth of Gold, *Imperialis*, &c.; but there are 269 species, many of which are very abundant in tropical seas as far south as the Cape. They are fond of warm pools, but are also found in deep water; they move slowly. There is one rather curious fact about the shell which I must ask you to take for granted, unless you will let me make a section of one of your Cones.'

'No, thank you. I have to take so many of your facts for granted that I don't think I shall hesitate to accept this. What is it?'

'Merely that the inner whorls are very much thinner than the outer one. It is supposed that the animal has reduced these *walls* (I don't wish to make a pun, but it is unavoidable) by absorbing some of their thickness, either to give itself more room, or to reduce the weight of the shell. There is one other genus included among the Cones—*Pleurotoma*, from *pleura*, a side, and *toma*, a notch; so named because there is a slit, or notch, in the right lip near the suture.'

'What do you mean by the suture?'

'The seam which marks one whorl from another in the spire. Pleurotoma is a spindle-shaped shell with a long, straight canal; it is a very large genus, containing over 400 species, and found all over the world. We have seventeen British species, so you see, though we have no Cones, the family is nevertheless represented in England. Now we come to the next family, the *Volutidæ*; this contains the Volutes, the Boat shells, the Mitres, and the Marginellas. The shells of this family are either turreted or convolute, the mouth is notched in front, and the under-lip is plaited obliquely; there is no operculum; all the animals have a very large foot, which partly hides the shell; the mantle, too, is often lobed and turned back over the shell; the eyes are either at the base of the tentacles or on them. Now, where is your *Voluta musica*, Poppy? That is the best type of the Volutes, perhaps; but they are some of the most beautiful shells known; they vary very much in shape and size; some are oval, some turreted, some spired, some globular, some are crowned with thorns——'

'Oh! Luke, what do you mean?'

'Why, they have a row of thorns or spines at the upper part of each whorl. Most of the Volutes are smooth and shining, with bright colours, beautifully varied. One very rare species has five or six white bands spotted with red on a dark ground.'

'Is that the rarest of the Volutes?'

'No. *Junonia* is the rarest; not more than four specimens of this are known, so it is rarer than, though not so valuable as, *Gloria maris*; it is yellowish white, covered with red-brown spots, dotted about it in various ways. Oh! there is *Musica*,' said Luke, taking up a shell marked with lines and spots so as to resemble a few bars of music.

'Let me see. How quaint it is! These plaits in

the columella are made by creases in the mantle, aren't they ? '

'Yes ; all the Volutes have that peculiarity. By the way, *Musica* is the only one that has an operculum ; there is no canal, you see ; and many species have an enormously wide mouth ; others are spindle-shaped, with a narrow mouth. The animal has a very flat, broad head, the tentacula wide apart, with eyes at the base ; the breathing tube is long and reflected. The Volutes like hot climates ; a few have been found in America, none in Europe ; some species grow to a very large size. The Boat shells, or *Cymba*, are a small genus ; there are only ten species ; those are found in West Africa and at Lisbon ; you may recognise them by the ill-shaped spire, and a sort of ledge which separates the body whorl and the outer lip. The animal has a very large foot ; the nucleus is large and irregular, and partly hidden by the growth of the shell.'

'What is the nucleus ? '

'All the Mollusca except the Argonaut have a rudimental shell before they are hatched. Very often it is a different shape and a different colour from the parent shell ; but it is the nucleus of the adult shell. In Cymba the animal is very large when born, which accounts for the large size of the nucleus ; a thin enamel is deposited upon the under side of the shell.'

'Now we come to these pretty Mitres. I think they are elegant and so beautifully proportioned.'

'So they are ; but, like some other beautiful things, their character is not so beautiful as their appearance ; for they are said to be poisonous, and to wound those who touch them with their pointed trunks.'

'I hope the boys won't get poisoned. They have gone down to the beach to look for shells this afternoon.'

'There is no fear. The Mitres don't honour our seas with their presence; most of them inhabit the Pacific, but there are 350 species, and some are found in the Mediterranean, though they prefer the tropics, and especially shallow water in the neighbourhood of coral-reefs. The animal has a small foot and head, a long breathing tube, and a very long proboscis, club-shaped at the end, from which it can throw out a purple liquid, which has a very unpleasant smell; if irritated, the animal ejects this fluid.'

'I am rather glad the Mitres are not English, notwithstanding their beauty, if they have such evil habits.'

'Now we have only one more genus, *Marginella*, and then we have done with the Volutes. The name means a little rim; some species are great favourites of mine; they are so beautifully polished and coloured. The animal covers the shell with its mantle; the spire is very short, and the right lip has the thickened margin which gives its name to the genus. And here we will stop for to-day. To-morrow we shall begin with the Cowries, though I have told you so much about them that there is not much left to say.'

'Thank you, Luke. I want you to tell me something before you go, please. If a shell is broken during the lifetime of a mollusc, does the animal always repair it?'

'That depends on the part which is broken. For instance, the apex is often injured or destroyed by boring worms and shells, and there is a sponge which can eat into the most solid shells. When this is the case, and when a hole is made far from the mouth, the animal is content with closing it with the viscid matter secreted by the mantle, but if the margin is broken, the animal can repair it perfectly, both in shape and colour, and also repair the epidermis.'

'Are shells always growing?'

'No; they cease growing in winter, and probably during the breeding season. This is why many shells are marked with lines of growth, and when the animal ceases to grow the shell does also.'

'Another thing I want to know is, does the form of the shell depend on the shape of the animal?'

'Not in the least; because the body of the mollusc is so soft and elastic that it can be doubled up into almost any shape. No, the form of the shell depends upon the way in which the mollusc protrudes the mantle; for instance, when the Limpet, which, as you know, is a basin-shaped shell, wants to enlarge its house, it puts out a little piece of mantle all round the rim of the basin; from the mantle exudes a liquid matter, which on exposure to the air or water becomes shell.'

'But how do they manage to make a spiral shell?'

'Well, that is harder to explain; but, in the first place, you know they only make one turn or whorl at a time; they protrude a little piece of the mantle from the mouth, but one side is more active than the other, consequently it stretches more. In most spirals you will find the whorls are turned towards the right; this is because the heart of most of the animals is on the left, and consequently the mantle is more active on the left side.'

'I think I understand. But now, how do bivalves grow?'

'Just in the same way. Each valve is enlarged at the same time. You may see the lines of growth here in this cockle, for instance.'

'And what makes the thorns and ridges on Murex and the Harps?'

'The mantle branches out, and divides into these spines or thorns in Murex; and the ridges are merely former mouths; for you will notice the outer lip is invariably thickened in all shells; even when the shell has finished growing outwardly it will continue to thicken this lip, and indeed the whole shell very often.'

'I don't think I shall ever understand how they manage to colour their shells so exquisitely.'

'Their food has something to do with it; the degree of heat they enjoy influences the colour, still more does the amount of light which reaches them. This is proved by the fact that bivalves which are very sedentary, and consequently only have the upper valve exposed to the air, are colourless on the under valve; the colour is also affected by the health of the animal.'

'Yes; but where does the colouring matter come from, and how does it get into the shell?'

'Poppy, what an Eve you are! But you are quite right to ask. The colouring matter is contained in the front part of the mantle only; and this is proved by the fact that if a shell be broken at any distance from the aperture, there is no colour in the repaired piece, but if broken at the margin the colour is reproduced as in the first instance. Very often the border of the mantle shows the same tints and patterns as those which adorn the shell. If you could see a living *Voluta undulata*, you would find this was the case.'

'Another thing I want to know, Luke, is, why the same species of shell—the common Whelk, for instance —is sometimes so thick and rough and heavy, and sometimes we find it quite thin and smooth ?'

'That depends upon the water they live in. If they live in rough, stormy seas the shells become rough and thick; when they live in still waters, the shells are thin and smooth. In the same way, the size of shells depends very much on the surrounding circumstances in which they are placed. If the situation is favourable, and they can obtain plenty of food, the animals grow to a large size, and the shells increase in proportion. On the other hand, if they are stinted in their food and live in places unfavourable to their growth, they do not attain so large a size.'

'Why, Luke, that is the tea-bell; it is seven o'clock ! How this afternoon has flown !'

'It has indeed! It can't be seven! Why, I don't believe the boys have come in yet !'

'I hope they have long ago. They went to the beach to look for shells, because it is a spring-tide. They must have come in. Why, it has been dark for an hour and a half !' said Poppy, as Luke wheeled her sofa into the dining-room, where Mr. and Mrs. Merton were already seated at the table.

'Where are the boys, my dear?' said Mrs. Merton.

'I thought they were in the drawing-room with Poppy and Luke.'

'No; I have not seen them since they went out at three o'clock. They have gone to the beach, mother. I do hope nothing has happened to them.'

'I'll go and inquire if they have come back. Very likely they got wet, and are changing their clothes,' said Luke.

But the boys, it soon appeared, had not been seen since they left the house; and, greatly alarmed, Mr. Merton and Luke hastily swallowed a cup of tea, for it was a very cold, raw evening, and then hurried out to look for them; leaving Mrs. Merton and Poppy to the much harder task of staying at home, wondering what had become of them, and fancying a hundred ills had befallen them.

'Oh! if I could only jump up and run out and look for them instead of lying here listening,' said Poppy.

'I wish you could with all my heart, dear; though it may be some comfort to you to know that I certainly should not allow you to run out on a cold night like this if you were able; and perhaps that would be even more trying than knowing you can't possibly go,' said Mrs. Merton, who was really more alarmed than she cared to let Poppy see.

An hour passed, and nothing was heard of the boys, though all the servants, and indeed half the village, were gone with lanterns to look for them. The clock on the dining-room chimney-piece, which chimed at the quarters, had struck half-past eight, when the hall door bell was violently rung, and Mrs. Merton rushed out to see who was there, followed by Poppy, who, cost her what it might, could not restrain her eagerness.

'Here we are! We have had a jolly time of it; didn't you wonder what had become of us? We are wet through, not a dry thread on us: it was a joke, and no mistake. We were in real danger part of the time, no nonsense about it, real danger!' exclaimed Robert.

'Real danger! I should just think we were; it was grand fun though. Hulloa! look at Poppy, she is fainting,' said Edward, as the pair entered the hall.

'Boys! boys! you have frightened us all terribly; help me with Poppy; there is no one else in the house, every one is gone to look for you.'

Somewhat sobered by this, and by Poppy's pale face and motionless form, the boys helped to move her on to her sofa, and then ran and fetched water, smelling-salts, and whatever else Mrs. Merton required. But even while they ran about waiting on her they could not restrain their excitement.

'Oh! mother, it was splendid; you know we were caught by the tide, we stopped too long on some rocks, and could not get back till it turned again. It was high water about six, and we got on these rocks before five; we were looking for shells, and did not notice the tide was so high till we found we were surrounded, and then we knew our only chance was to wait till it turned again,' said Robert.

'Here's the eau-de-cologne, mother; she is coming

round. Oh! we have had an adventure; there we had to cling on like grim death to a rock for what seemed ages, but I suppose it wasn't more than a quarter of an hour, and the spray came over us, and we thought every moment a wave would wash us off.'

'Be quiet, boys! you will frighten Poppy into another fainting-fit; go and ring the big bell, to let them all know you are found.'

'Then we'll change our clothes, and have a good supper—I am ravenous,' said Robert.

'So am I; here is father,' said Edward, as Mr. Merton, looking dreadfully anxious, came in.

'Thank God you are safe then! where have you been?'

'We have had splendid fun; we have been in real danger, father,' began both boys.

'Hush, send the boys away, dear, to change their wet clothes. Poppy has fainted; it has been too much for her.'

'Go to bed this moment, both of you; and you may think yourselves very lucky if I don't follow you up, and give you each a good flogging—alarming us all in this way, and taking it as coolly as possible,' said Mr. Merton angrily.

The boys subsided after this, and retired to their own room, very hungry and very crestfallen, to find that a thrashing was hanging over their heads, instead of the supper they had reckoned on. However, they dare not make any excuses, so up they went, solacing themselves with a good grumble when they got to their own rooms. But as soon as Poppy had recovered consciousness,

Mrs. Merton's thoughts reverted to her boys, whom she had no intention of allowing to go supperless to bed after spending two or three hours in wet clothes.

'Those boys must have some hot soup and a fire in their room, and a hot bath; I'll go and see after them, dear, if you and Poppy will take care of each other, otherwise they'll take cold.'

'Very well, dear; you shall have your way to-night; to-morrow morning I'll punish them both severely; and you may tell them so. I have strictly forbidden them ever to go on those rocks unless Luke or I am with them; it is a piece of gross disobedience.'

'I think they forgot, father; they were looking for shells for me, so you must let them off for my sake,' said Poppy, coaxing her father's head with her hand.

'Forgetfulness is no excuse; but I will sleep upon it. I feel very angry with them to-night. Here is Luke, so we will have some supper after our exertions; I think we deserve it as much as those young monkeys whom your mother is pampering so up there.'

The next morning, very much to the relief of the boys, Mr. Merton did not appear to breakfast, but had his sent to his room, as he had had a bad night.

'Father isn't ill, is he, mother?' said Poppy anxiously.

'No, dear; only very tired.'

'I thought I heard a noise in the house last night, but I was so dreadfully sleepy I could not rouse myself to go and see what it was; did you hear anything, Mrs. Merton?' said Luke Thorne.

'Yes, it was Mr. Merton and I; the fact is—for perhaps I had better let you all into the secret, lest you find it out for yourselves and get a fright into the bargain—your father occasionally walks in his sleep, and he did so last night.'

'Walks in his sleep, mother! do you mean he is a somnambulist?' asked Poppy.

'Yes; he has not done it for a long time, perhaps because I often stop him, but if he has had any unusual excitement he is apt to attempt it; and last night I got up to go and peep at Poppy, feeling anxious about her, and when I came back I found your father was not in the room. I guessed he was walking in his sleep, and went to look for him. I found him just outside the drawing-room door, sound asleep; he was unlocking the door, and between us we dropped the key, which was perhaps the noise you heard, Luke, though we probably made a noise on the stairs.'

'Did father wake when you spoke to him?'

'No, dear, not until we got back to our own room; then he did, but he lay awake for ever so long afterwards, trying to remember what he was dreaming of, and wondering what he could have been going to do in the drawing-room.'

'I wish you had let him go on, mother; you might have followed, to see he did not break anything,' said Poppy.

'I might, but I was not curious, only very cold, and anxious to get back to bed. Your father is rather proud of his somnambulistic achievements; but I don't care to encourage them, I am so afraid of his hurting himself. However, he was quite vexed with me for bringing him back last night.'

'Bad look out for us, if he is in a bait this morning,' said Robert in an undertone to Edward.

But whether Poppy's intercession was the cause, or whether Mr. Merton was more mercifully disposed in the morning, he let them off with an imposition.

CHAPTER VII.

CONCERNS SHELLS ONLY.

'The Lord hath made all things for Himself.'—Prov. xvi. 4.

'All things that are forked, and horned, and soft,
  In the purple twilights—under the sea.'—Tennyson.

'Luke, how is it Cowries have no spire?' said Poppy, the next time Luke was ready to give her a lesson.

'I am glad you asked me that, Poppy; the truth is, they have a spire, and in the young shell a very prominent one, covered with a thin epidermis; but this is concealed entirely in the full-grown Cowry by the lobes of the mantle, which expand on each side and deposit a thin coating of shining enamel. Give me one of your Cowries a moment, Poppy; look, do you see this line of paler colouring? This is where the mantle-lobes meet; you may see it on nearly all Cowries. There is a sub-genus where the plaits of the outer lip are continued over the margin of the canal; and there are two other genera, *Erato* and *Ovulum.* There is nothing much to say of the first; Ovulum, as its name implies, for it is the diminutive form of *ovum*, an egg, is egg-shaped; both shell and animal are very like the Cowry.'

'Have not I a shell called the Weaver's Shuttle?'

'Yes; that is an Ovulum, with a long canal at each end; it feeds on the round stems of a plant, and has a foot specially adapted to crawling round them. Now, we come to the Sea Snails, the second section of the first order of the class Gasteropoda. These are mostly plant-feeders; the shell is either spiral or limpet-shaped, very seldom bivalve; the mouth has no notch, which is a sign, but not an infallible one, that the animals are vegetable-feeders. The operculum is shelly, or at least horny, and generally spiral; the animals have a short muzzle, and no breathing-tube; their eyes are placed at the base of the tentacles. There are fifteen families, including among others the Periwinkles, the Turret shells, the Top shells, the Ear shells, the Limpets, and the Chitons.'

'Do let us begin with the Chitons, please, Luke; I am so curious to hear about them.'

'They are generally put at the end, instead of the beginning, of the Sea Snails; but you know I would do anything in the world to please you, so with the Chitons we will begin.'

'No, I don't know that,' said Poppy, laughing and blushing; 'you don't always let me do as I like. You took away one of my dear shell books yesterday, when I wanted to go on reading it.'

'Because you were tiring yourself, and would not leave off to please me.'

'Ah! that is another thing; we were talking of

I

pleasing me, not of pleasing you; but now go on with
the Chitons. You looked as stern as father does
sometimes, when you carried off my Woodward; I mean
to have a lot of indulgences out of you to make up for
that.'

Luke coloured up to the roots of his hair, and bit
his lip, as he said, almost sharply,.

'Well, now, about the Chitons. The shell is made of
eight small pieces, which overlap each other, and are
united by a tough ligament, which is sometimes smooth
and fleshy, sometimes wrinkled, sometimes scaly, or
hairy; and in a few species it is armed with thin, long,
black spines. The entire shell is something like a boat
in shape, and the inside is generally white; but one
species is lined with a beautiful rose-colour, others have
a green lining. The animals can roll themselves and
their shells up into a ball, like a hedgehog. They are
found in all climates throughout the world; we have a
few British species, smaller in size than the tropical
Chitons, which often measure several inches. They are
found at low water on rocks and stones, to which they
stick like a limpet; they can move if they choose about
the stalks of plants very quickly, turning their bodies
from right to left; but during the day they are
generally quiet, and if disturbed, they move away in a
slow and dignified manner, if they don't wax sulky,
and roll themselves up into a ball. At night, however,
when they usually feed, they quicken their pace. I
hope you have observed, Poppy, how careful I have been
to avoid all scientific terms in my description of the
Chitons ?'

Yes; and it is lucky for you, you were. How many species are there?'

'Over two hundred. The animals are blind, and have neither eyes nor tentacles; they have a long toothed tongue, and a long foot or creeping disk. And now, having satisfied your curiosity on the subject of these marine coats-of-mail, may I be permitted to begin with *Naticidæ*, the first family on my list?'

'Oh yes! those pretty little Naticas.'

'*Natica* is only one of the genera; there are four others, but we will only pass lightly over the others. All the family have globular shells, with a small spire and very few whorls. The mouth is like a half-moon in shape; the animal is blind, and has a very large foot, and the mantle-lobes are also large, and hide more or less of the shell. In *Natica*, the shell is thick and smooth, and the colours are remarkably permanent, and are often preserved in fossil specimens. The animal is very large in proportion to the shell, and has several appendages; the foot, which is large, has a flap which turns back and protects the head, and the operculum has a lobe which covers part of the shell, while the head has two horns. These animals are carnivorous, unlike most of this section. The genus *Narica* has some very pretty little shells, thin, white-ribbed and cross-barred; in *Lamellaria* the shell is entirely concealed by the mantle, and the animal is much larger than the shell. On the whole, I don't think them an interesting family. We will go on to the Pyramid shells. These all have a turreted spire and a small mouth; the animals have eyes behind the tentacles, they are all marine; but the day for Pyramids is passed, they are a falling family, the present members being liliputian in comparison with many fossil specimens, so they are perhaps more interesting to geologists than to conchologists.'

' Oh no, Luke ; I think they are dear, pretty little shells.'

' Then of course I meekly bow to your decision ; but all the same I don't think there is much to tell you about them. One genus, of which we have several British species, is called *Euluna*, from a Greek word meaning ravenous hunger. The shell is small, slender, white, and polished, and former mouths are faintly indicated on one side ; inside, these mouths form prominent ribs ; the animal creeps along with its head hidden inside the aperture, the tentacles peeping out, but its foot much in advance of these. The *Cerites* form the next family ; these are spiral shells with many whorls, and the mouth channelled in front and slightly at the back ; the operculum is horny and spiral. The animals have eyes fixed on little horns, not on the tentacles. The prettiest genus is fossil ; another, called the Fresh-water Cerites, is so abundant that in some places, Calcutta, for instance, the shells are used for burning into lime. I think we may pass over the *Melaniadæ*, and go on to the Turret shells.'

' What a hurry you are in to-day, Luke !'

' No; I am only hurrying over the least interesting genera, or else I shall never get through with all these families before I leave to be ordained.'

' But that won't be for another year, will it ?'

' No ; but see how many interruptions we have in various ways. I want to finish the Gasteropoda before

Easter, if possible, so now listen.   The Precious Wentle
Trap, or *Scalaria pretiosa*, is the most interesting of the
Turret shells; the genus, I should tell you, is called *Scalaria*,

THE PRECIOUS WENTLE TRAP SHELL.

or a ladder, in English Wentle Trap. *Pretiosa* is only one
species; it comes from China and Japan; the common
Wentle Trap is found on our coasts, and they all give

out a purple fluid if attacked.   The Turritellas, or Little
Towers, are pretty turreted shells; in some foreign species
the whorls vary from fifteen to thirty in number, and
the shells grow to four or five inches long; the full-
grown animal does not inhabit the whole of his tower,
but partitions off the upper story; it is not certain
whether they are vegetable-feeders or carnivorous.'

'Oh! carnivorous, I should think, Luke; look, the
mouth is notched in this *Cathedralis.*'

'Well, perhaps he was an old abbot, and gave himself
a dispensation to eat meat.   One genus, *Cerithium*, is
remarkable for the power of fasting the animals possess;
not only that, but they can live for a long time if taken
out of the water.   The whorls of this genus are generally
covered with spines or prickles, which form beautiful
architectural designs.   There is one living species,
Giganteum, which is more than a foot long, and the only
known specimen, which was fished up off the Australian
coast by an English sailor, belongs to a Frenchman.
There are fossil specimens larger than this.   These
shells are marine, though some frequent salt marshes
and the mouths of rivers, and some have been found
hanging by silken threads to the branches of trees.
Another genus of the Turret shells is *Vermetus*, or
Worm shell.   There is only one living species, and very
curious it is; it is an irregular spiral tube twisted about
like a worm, except just the spire; the mouth is round,
with the lips united; great numbers twisted together are
often found in the African seas, but they also exist in the
Mediterranean.   A similar genus is *Siliquaria ;* this is
found in sponges in the Mediterranean and in Australian

seas. The next family are the Periwinkles, in science *Litorinidœ*, that means inhabiting the shore; they are rather a large family, but by far the commonest genus is the *Litorina*, or Periwinkle.'

'You told me a great deal about them in your lecture.'

'I think I did; but I don't think I told you tha there is one species, a sort of first - cousin of the common periwinkle, which moves in a higher sphere living in a region where it is rarely reached by the tide; it is not eaten, because the young, which are produced alive, have a hard shell before their birth. In the Baltic periwinkles frequently become distorted, like many of our fossil specimens. To this family belongs a genus called in Latin *Solarium*, which means a dial, but the English name is the Staircase shell.'

'In this case I think the Latin name much the best; it is far more like a sun-dial than a staircase. One of my specimens is beautifully marked with black and yellow; are there any British species?'

'No; they come from tropical seas. The Carrier shells, or *Phorus*, are rather a quaint genus; they carry stones, or corals, or other shells on the margin of their own shells; these they attach as they grow, and they are called by collectors "Mineralogists," or "Conchologists," according to the substance they carry. The shell is shaped like a top, with flat whorls; little is known of the habits of the animal, but it is said to frequent rough bottoms, and to scramble about like the Strombs. I must not forget to mention a minute genus, called *Rissoa*, after a French naturalist, for it contains some very lovely little shells, beautiful both in shape and colour, and no less than twenty-eight species are found on our sands.'

'How I wish I were well, and able to go and look for them! It is no use setting the boys to go and look for tiny little things like those; they seem to think the whole value of a shell depends on its size—the bigger it is the more valuable.'

'I know; I'll go and look for some for you. They are to be found on sea-weed near the shore. I should like you to see the living animal; it has long slender tentacles, with eyes at their base, and a pointed foot; in one species the eyes are only visible through the transparent shell; many are fastened to the sea-weed by threads. The family are river-snails, so we will leave them and pass on to the *Neritidæ*, or Sea Snail; these have thick semi-globular shells, with a very small spire, and only one chamber, the partitions having been absorbed by the animal, who apparently prefers to live in one room; on each end of the columella,—what is the columella, Poppy?' said Luke, breaking off.

'The left or inner lip.'

'Right; well, you may recognise this family by an oblong muscular impression at each end of the columella. The animal has long slender tentacles, and two shorter stalks or horns, which bear the eyes, a broad muzzle, and a triangular foot. The first genus, the *Nerites*, or Sea Snails, inhabit warm seas; they have a horny epidermis: some of them are beautifully marked and ornamented with spots, lines and bands; these are worn by the Indians as ornaments. One species is called the "bleeding tooth," because it has a red stain on the inner lip. The river shells are prettier than the marine, and are usually placed in another genus; both are remarkable for their opercula, which turn very much like a door on its hinges; there are two other genera, but they are not very interesting. The Top shells, or *Turbinidæ*, come next; these are all marine, feeding on sea-weed; when the epidermis and outer coat are removed, the Top shells are all brilliantly pearly. Sometimes quite a golden hue is cast over them; particularly is this the case with *Turbo*, or Whipping Top; this genus comes from warm seas. The Pheasant shells, or *Phasianella*, belong to the Top family; they are polished and richly coloured. The handsomest species, which are crimson and brown and purple, come from Australia. The animal is as brilliant a creature as his shell; the shape is an elongated top. Formerly these were very rare shells, and they are still very valuable and prized by collectors, particularly the Indian and Australian species.'

'Is there a British species?'

'Yes, a very small one; but it is very pretty and beautifully marked, it is very common in Guernsey. The genus *Trochus*, which means a hoop, contains some very handsome shells; their shape is conical or pyramidal, with a flat base, with a very nacreous aperture.'

'Pearly mouth, Luke; that is much prettier than nacreous aperture,' interrupted Poppy.

'Well, it is equally beautiful by either name; we have sixteen British species, but though very iridescent, they are neither so large nor so beautiful as the tropical species; they are generally to be found near low water under sea-weed and stones. Some of the genera have such long names, I dare not even broach them to you; but I must not omit *Delphinula*, or the Dolphins, for they are very curious, and sometimes very beautiful; they are all found on reefs at low water in the Indian Ocean. The shell is very strong and thick, and rolled up into an almost indescribable shape, with a depressed spire and few whorls; it has a pearly mouth; the animal is like Turbo and Trochus, only it has no head-lobes.'

'Oh, now you are coming to the Ear shells,' said Poppy, as Luke took out a drawer of Ear shells from a cabinet.

'Yes; now I want you particularly to notice this horse-shoe mark, it is a muscular impression; do you see it?'

'Yes; but, Luke, how lovely the colours of the pearly lining are; how I should like to see the living animal, with its mantle peeping out through these holes!'

'You would see a blue-eyed creature, with a body of brown, green, salmon-pink, and white. In Guernsey they decorate their cottage-gardens with these Ormer shells; and in the South Sea Islands they make a musical instrument out of them, also fish-hooks and spoons, and they decorate their boats with them. Another genus, called *Stomatia*, is like the Ormer, only the shell has no holes, but a simple furrow in its place. These shells are found at low water, in the Pacific Islands, under stones; we have one minute British genus, but only found in deep water; there are several fossil genera, and last, but not least, the lovely *Ianthina*, or Violet Snail, belongs to this family.'

'I can't see how the Violet Snail is related to the Ear shells.'

'It is not a true Haliotid; but Woodward includes it in this family, because of its notched mouth. But I have described both the animal and its shell to you in my lecture; so we will go on to the Limpets, of which there are three distinct families. We will begin with the *Fissurellidæ*, or Keyhole Limpets; so called because the hole at the apex of the shell, which is conical or basin-shaped, like all the limpets, is sometimes like a keyhole. In some species it is round or oblong; in very young species the apex is entire, but this hole gradually increases with the growth of the animal until the spire is worn quite away.'

'What is the use of the hole?'

'To let out the water from the animal's gills. Both shell and animal are remarkable for their symmetry. The Keyhole Limpets proper, that is, the genus *Fissurella*, move about; there are 150 species, a few of which are British, and are found in the same places as Patella; the shells are thick and strong, and some tropical species are beautifully marked, and painted in coloured rays. The genus *Emarginula*, named from a Latin word meaning notched, has a narrow slit on the front margin, which varies very much in size in different species; the shell of the fry is spiral; there are three British species. The shell of the Duck's Bill Limpet is a very long oblong, but a very short duck's bill; it is smooth and white; the animal is black, and very much larger than the shell; it can, and does, walk about in shallow water, but it is tropical.'

' Is that the end of the Keyhole Limpets ? '

'Yes ; now we come to the Bonnet Limpets, which, to my mind, are much more like hats and caps than bonnets, though I speak with all humility on so profound a question—only to be solved by the feminine mind. The Bonnet Limpets are most sedentary animals, many of them never leaving the place they first settle on, usually a rock or a stone, which is very often found worn away beneath their feet. Their shape and colour depend very much on the situation in which they grow.'

' What do they feed on, if they never move ? '

'It is supposed on animalculæ, or the sea-weed round them. The Bonnet Limpet, or *Pileopsis*, from two Greek words, *opsis*, like, and *pileos*, a cap, is also called the Hungarian Bonnet, which it very much resembles in shape ; it is found on oysters. A few species of the Cup and Saucer Limpet are found in England ; it is so named from a cup-like projection on the inside of the shell. One curious genus is *Crepidula*, or Sandal ; it is very like a small sandal in shape ; they are sedentary animals, often found sticking to each other in groups ; living and dead together. Some species inhabit empty spiral shells, and are themselves colourless, very thin, and nearly flat. *Crepidula onyx* is a brilliant black inside, while the toe of the sandal is white. Other species are parasites, and are carried about on the shells they live on.'

' Then, if I were a limpet, I should like to be a parasite, instead of spending all my life on a rock. I think, as it is, my life is very like a limpet's, glued to this sofa.'

'Don't, Poppy; I can't bear to hear you complain, and know I can do nothing for you; but you are not to spend your life on that sofa, you know.'

'I shall have to spend another twelve months here, though, I am nearly sure. But never mind me, go on with the real limpets.'

'I am now coming to them; you know the shell so well I need not describe it. The animal has a distinct head with tentacles, and eyes at their base; the foot is the same size as the outer margin of the shell; but I told you all I thought likely to interest you about them in that lecture. I don't think the arrangement of their breathing apparatus—a favourite topic among naturalists—would interest you.'

'Not in the least; so now have we finished with the Limpets?'

'Yes; and with the exception of the Tooth shells, about which there is not much to say, we have finished with the first section of the Gasteropoda. The *Dentalium* are curious shells in shape, like a long single tooth with its fang; they are found in sand and mud, in which they bury, and they are animal-feeders: and now I am sure you are tired, so we will have done with Conchology for to-day.'

And Poppy did not deny it, though the lesson was not all given in one day, as reported in this chapter for convenience sake.

The Nautilus

CHAPTER VIII

THE FATE OF POPPY'S PAPER NAUTILUS.

'Let the heaven and earth praise Him, the seas, and everything that moveth therein.'—PSALM LXIX. 34.

'Spread, tiny Nautilus, the living sail;
Dive at thy choice, or brave the freshening gale.'
WORDSWORTH.

EASTER had come and gone, the summer was over; and during all these months, from one reason or another, Luke and Poppy had had no more conchological lessons, and, what is stranger, nothing had been heard of *Gloria maris;* that mystery had never been solved, but remained still a mystery. They often talked of it, and wondered what had become of it, in Mr. Merton's absence; but the subject was one which worried him exceedingly, so it was seldom mentioned before him. Mr. Dobson was so much put out by his own failure to discover any clue which might lead to its recovery, that he spent ten days in lodgings with his wife and family in the village during the month of August, and pro-secuted a great many inquiries during his so-called holiday, but with no better result than in the previous November.

But although *Gloria maris* was lost, and the lessons had ceased for a time, Poppy's love of shells had increased very much. She had taught herself a great deal about them from her books, and her collection had been added to by Luke Thorne and the boys, who rarely went for a scramble over the rocks without bringing her back some specimens. Often Poppy found she already possessed them, on looking at her cabinets; but sometimes the specimens were new to her, and then her delight fully repaid Luke and the boys for any trouble they might have taken.

It was true that during the summer, what with tennis and cricket and other out-door amusements, Luke had not much time to teach Poppy; but his real reason for postponing the lessons was, he found it very hard to be alone with her so much as the lessons necessitated, and not tell her how dear she was to him; and there were many reasons why he could not do this. In the first place, she was still very young; then her health was a great drawback, while he was scarcely in a position to engage himself; and if he did win Poppy, and gain her father's consent, he was quite certain that it would only be on condition that he left the Rectory at once, and found some one else to read with. This he by no means wished to do; for if all went well he hoped to be ordained either at Christmas or the following Easter, and until then he wished to remain with Mr. Merton; so he resolved to avoid Poppy as much as possible, and on no account to say anything to her about his love; and so the shell-lessons remained in abeyance. But they were destined to be resumed somewhat abruptly, for one day Poppy had a letter from Arthur Graham, saying he had sent her home a box of shells, which ought to arrive about the same time as the letter. The box did not, however, turn up for a few days, and the excitement as to its contents was very great, not only in the case of Poppy but also of the boys, with whom Arthur was a prime favourite. Luke Thorne perhaps would have been as well pleased if the shells had not been sent, and did not show the impatience of the rest of the family for their arrival.

However, they arrived at last one morning. It happened to be All Saints' Day. Poppy, who was only allowed to go to church on Sundays and festivals, was gone with her mother, on her movable couch, and the two boys were left at home to prepare their lessons. The arrival of a parcel was, of course, a signal for them to shut up their books and run out and see what it was; and when they found it was the shells from Arthur Graham, and that it would be at least half an hour before the others came out of church, they decided to open it. Their impatience was so great that they could not restrain their curiosity, and Poppy would not be able to open it herself in any case; so, as the box was nailed down, they put it on the dining-room table, and fetching chisels and hammers, prepared to open it. Perhaps they were not very clever carpenters; perhaps their impatience made them careless; at any rate, they bungled a good deal over it, and finally, when the lid was nearly off, the chisel Edward was working with slipped, and went down into the box, striking against some object, which it evidently broke to atoms, for a slight crash was heard.

'Hullo! We have broken something,' said Robert.

'I have, you mean,' said Edward dolefully.

'Well, it is as much my fault as yours. Your chisel happened to be the one, instead of mine; but that was a fluke.'

'I wish we had let it alone,' said Edward.

'So do I. However, let us see what the damage is, said Robert, diving into a mass of hay and cotton wool as soon as he had wrenched the lid off the box.

'Now, you boys, what are you up to? Some mischief, I'll be bound. What is the meaning of all this hammering during school hours?' said Luke Thorne, bursting suddenly into the room.

'I thought you were gone to church with the others, said Edward.

'Well, I am not, you see. What is that box, pray?'

'Poppy's shells from Arthur Graham. We are opening it for her.'

K

'With her consent, of course. But I wonder she trusted you two to do it; it is rather a delicate task.'

'She didn't trust us; she is at church. She does not know the shells have come.'

'Then what business have you to touch them? I never heard of such impertinence! Put the lid on, and let me carry the box to the drawing-room; it sha'n't be touched till Poppy comes home.'

'I wish we had not touched it. We have broken something — at least, I have; I heard it crash,' said Edward.

'You'll both have a very pleasant quarter of an hour when your father comes in then, my friends,' said Luke grimly, as he carried the box into the next room.

Shortly after, Poppy was wheeled back from church —which was just outside the garden gate—by Luke and her father, and on reaching the house the boys met her, and told her what had happened.

'We thought you would not mind our opening the box, Poppy; but I wish we hadn't, for we have broken something.'

'Whatever you have broken you must pay for out of your pocket-money. You had no business to touch the box,' said Mr. Merton sternly.

'We will see what is broken. Perhaps there is not much damage done after all,' said Poppy.

But when Luke, by her request, began to unpack the box, it was found that the broken shell was a Paper Nautilus, into which Edward's chisel had been driven, smashing it to pieces.

'Oh! it is a Paper Nautilus! What a thousand pities!' said Luke.

'Well, it can't be helped. I am evidently not meant to have an Argonaut. They say there are men who can't own a black horse; evidently I can't own a Paper Nautilus,' said Poppy.

'Nonsense, my dear child; you would have owned one to-day, but for the mischievous propensities of your brothers. However, I stop your pocket-money until you have bought Poppy another. Now go back to your lessons; you sha'n't see the box unpacked. You have seen the mischief you have done—let that suffice.'

The boys retired very crestfallen, and Luke went on unpacking the shells. There were some Cowries, one or two Murexes, some beautiful Pectens, some Strombs, and a box full of minute shells, which would have to be identified later on; but the Argonaut was the gem of the box, and the very one Poppy most wished for.

'With all due deference to Graham, I think it was very stupid of him not to put such a fragile shell as Argonauta into a small box,' said Luke.

'It would have been wiser; but still, if the box had been properly unpacked, it would have travelled safely enough, no doubt,' said Mr. Merton.

'Well, I am very glad to have these shells. They are a very nice addition to my collection, and if I have duplicates of any, I can send them up to Sowerby, and he'll exchange them for others, or let them go towards a Paper Nautilus. Luke, we must begin our lessons again at once; these shells have given me a fresh spur;

K 2

so we'll begin this very day, please. I mean to have a holiday, and spend it among my shells. I shall have to look through my collection, to find the proper place for these new ones.'

Luke raised no objection. Indeed, probably, in his heart of hearts, he was as glad as Poppy to renew their lessons; so that afternoon he came into the drawing-room with the tea, and took up his subject where he had left it six months before.

'We had finished the first order of the Gasteropoda, the Prosobranchiata, or Molluscs which breathe through gills. We now come to the second order, the *Pulmoni-fera*, or air-breathing molluscs; most of these are land-snails, some are slugs, about which you won't want to hear much; some inhabit fresh waters, none are really marine, though a few inhabit salt-marshes or fag-ends of rivers. But although you have no land-shells in your collection, I may as well just mention a few, which are specially interesting; shall I?'

'Yes, please; tell me about the Roman Snail, which is found in England wherever there are Roman ruins.'

'Wherever the Romans formerly lived; it is a large light-brown snail, called *Helix Pomatia*; they used to eat them, and it is supposed that they fed them up for this purpose, just as in Brittany, Switzerland, and some parts of Germany they fatten snails up for food now; on the shores of the Mediterranean they are largely eaten, boiled with rice.'

'There is a tradition which says,—excuse my interrupting you, Luke,' said Mr. Merton, who was present,—that snails formed part of the food of the children of

Israel in their journey to the Promised Land, for travellers report that in the desert and its neighbourhood large quantities of very large snails are met with.'

'Thank you, sir; I believe they are sold in England to be boiled in milk, and eaten in cases of consumption; and I know the Americans send them over here as a delicacy—perhaps because they don't care about them themselves. In England snails remain in a torpid state throughout the winter; they dislike cold very much, and fortify themselves against it by closing the mouths of their shells with a sort of covering or door, called an *epiphragma*; sometimes they make two or three of these doors, which are not attached to the animal, like the operculum, but can be thrown over when the spring comes. Some snails bury themselves in the earth during the winter; our common garden snails creep into crevices in a bunch or cluster.'

'How do they manage to breathe through these doors?'

'There is a very tiny hole in the door, which communicates with the hinges; this admits sufficient air to enable them to breathe during their torpid state, when their respiration is exceedingly slow. They can exist on a minimum of air and food apparently, for snails that have been shut up for years in a cabinet have been found alive when put in warm water; instances have occurred of two snails which were shut up in pill-boxes without any food for two years and a half, and were found alive at the end of that time.'

'I wish boys were like snails; they are almost as tenacious of life; but how delightful it would be if we could shut Robert and Edward up in a box for two years, and find them none the worse for it, wouldn't it, Poppy?' said Mr. Merton.

'No, father; you know it would not. But, Luke, I want to know if snails can mend their shells if they get broken?'

'Yes; not only can they mend their shells, but they can mend their bodies also; if their head, for instance, is cut off, they will grow a new one. It takes some months, it is true, to grow a new head, and they have to remain indoors during the process, but they can do it. There is a beautiful genus of snails found in all parts of the world, called *Bulimus*. The shell is oval and turreted, the body whorl very large, and in some tropical species the shells grow to a large size, and are beautifully coloured with rare colours for shells, such as lemon, sea-green, and amber. At Rio Janeiro they are six inches long, and are sold in the market for food. These snails place their eggs, which are sometimes as large as a pigeon's, among dead leaves, cemented together, and when hatched the young are an inch long. They remain dormant during the winter, and in the spring they bury themselves in the sand, and lay their eggs about two inches below the surface.'

'Have we any British species?' asked Poppy.

'Oh, yes, several; there are thirty European species. I don't know how many are British, it is a very large genus; there are 650 species. In Cornwall, a species called *Acutus* is very plentiful, and is very useful in helping to fatten the sheep, which feed in the sandy pastures near the sea, which Bulimus prefers as his home. All the genus seems to have a hankering after the sea, for they are most frequently found on islands, or on rocks or trees close to the sea. But the largest known land shells are the *Achatinæ*, or Agate shells. We have two small British species, generally found at the roots of trees in limestone districts, like Bulimus. Many of them are reversed or left-handed shells. One species, *Columnaris*, is always reversed, and the columella forms a winding column, which reaches to the top of the spire, and makes it one of the most remarkable of land shells. The great African Achatinæ are eight inches long. Their eggs are over an inch long; they always live near water and near trees, and are very plentiful at the Cape of Good Hope. Now, Poppy, we come to the Slugs; do you wish to hear anything about them?'

'I wish to hear how to exterminate them,' said Mr. Merton.

'I don't care to hear anything about them; they have no shell. I can think of nothing but shells to-day, Luke,' said Poppy.

'Very well, we'll leave the slugs then; but they have an internal shell, and they have a mantle, under which they hide their heads if frightened. We'll go on to the Pond Snails, or *Limnæidæ*; these have a thin horn-coloured shell, spiral in shape; they frequent fresh water in all parts of the world, but they seem to prefer stagnant water to rivers; they glide about under water with their shell downwards, and hybernate in the mud.'

'Horrid creatures! I don't care much for them.'

'We'll go on to the *Auriculidæ*, then; these used

formerly to be considered marine shells, but they frequent salt-marshes and places within reach of the sea chiefly. The name means "a little ear." The shells are spiral, and covered with a horny epidermis. The mouth of *Auricula* is toothed on both lips. This closes the first section of Land Snails. The second, or Operculated Snails, are very like periwinkles, and not interesting. I am not sure whether Poppy, having such a dislike to slugs, will consider the Sea Slugs worthy of her notice; for when they have a shell it is thin and small, and generally partly, if not entirely concealed by the animal. The first family, the *Tornatellas*, are mostly extinct, so I won't worry you with them; but I will just say a few words about the Bubble shells, or *Bulla*, for they are sea shells, and you have some in your collection.'

'Is it an egg-shaped shell, rolled up in a funny way?'

'Yes, Bulla itself is. The animal is much bigger than the shell, but only partially covers it, and it can very nearly squeeze itself into its shell; it swims very well with the side lobes of its mantle. It is a very voracious animal, sometimes swallowing other shells as big as itself, so that it is blown out to a great size.'

'How does it manage to digest such a dinner?' asked Mr. Merton.

'It has some internal arrangement, very like the gizard of a bird, which enables it to do so. I believe it can be seen shining through the shell. Another genus, *Scaphanda*, or Boatman, has the same power. The Sea Hares, which are the third family of this order—

Opisthobranchiata; a long word, Poppy, meaning that the gills are placed in the hinder part of the body—the Sea Hares, or *Aphysia*, live chiefly on sea-weed, but very often vary their diet with animal food; the animals are like slugs, with a small, thin, transparent shell or shield, which covers the gills, and is covered by the mantle. The Sea Hares are quite harmless, and if you could overcome your disgust sufficiently, and handled them, they would not hurt you, Poppy; the worst they could do would be to throw out a violet fluid, which could not do you the slightest harm, and which changes to a red colour; if they emit this fluid in the sea, the water is coloured for a foot round it. Formerly the Sea Hares were looked upon as objects of dread, partly on account of their queer shape, and partly because this pretty violet fluid was supposed to be poisonous, and to produce ineradicable stains. One species is found on our coasts; the eggs are placed among sea-weed, and are often joined together in long ribbons.'

'Does the Umbrella shell belong to the Sea Hares?'

'No; to the next family, the *Pleurobranchidæ*, from *pleura*, a side, and *branchia*, a gill. These have gills in their sides; they have very complicated digestive organs, but live on vegetable food; they have a limpet-like shell, often concealed. The *Umbrella Indica*, or Chinese Parasol, is the best known; it is found in the Indian Ocean, and is shaped like an umbrella; it is thin and transparent, with ribs radiating from the centre. The next section, called *Nudibranchiata*, have no shell; this includes, among many others, the Sea Lemons and Sea Nymphs; but they are all creatures of too slug-like

a nature to interest Poppy in any way, so I will pass
them over, and go on to the *Nucleobranchiata*—that is,
animals whose gills are arranged in a nucleus. They
all swim on the surface of the sea, and are called
pelagic; the animals and shells are both symmetrical,
and there are only two families : the *Firolas*, which
have large bodies and (if any) small shells, and the
Atlantas, which have shells large enough for them to
retire into entirely, and, having retired, they possess a
door to close them with.'

'You mean they have an operculum ?'

'Just so. These Molluscs have a fin-like sail instead
of a foot, like ordinary Molluscs; with this they swim
about in the open sea, generally at night, and they
prefer warm climates; their bodies are transparent, and,
as a rule, have no colour; their probable food is other
Molluscs, but what they live on is not certainly known,
but their mouth is provided with horny hooks for
tearing their prey. Sometimes they have eyes, sometimes they have not, and the same may be said with
regard to their feelers—indeed, they appear to be able
to get on just as comfortably without heads as with
them. They are very restless, and seem to be always
swimming, though they can and do attach themselves
to sea-weed with their tail, which is provided, for that
purpose, with a small sucker; they are seen by millions,
sometimes for several nights in succession, swimming
about in the open sea. *Carinaria*, a genus of the *Firola*
family, has a very thin, transparent, glassy shell, in shape
not unlike a miniature fireman's helmet; the animal is
most brilliantly coloured, but only shows itself in a calm

sea. Small as these shells are, they used to be very valuable, and as much as a hundred guineas have been given for *Carinaria vitrea*, which is found in the African seas. There is one species which is so small— about the size of a grain of sand—that it requires a microscope to reveal its beauties; and yet, tiny as it is, it has some very vicious tendencies, for it sometimes feeds on its smaller brothers and sisters.'

'I should not care to possess such an ignoble atom,' said Poppy.

'Perhaps you would prefer a tiny *Atlanta*, for there is one very minute species — *Pervina* — which is very beautiful; it is glassy, keeled, and spiral, transparent, and small; but small as it is, it is large enough to contain the animal. I believe you have some, by the way; I'll see. And as we have now finished with the Gasteropoda, we had better leave off for to-day, and start fresh with the next class to-morrow.'

CHAPTER IX.

NEPTUNE'S BUTTERFLIES, LAMP SHELLS AND PEARLS.

'All things were made by Him, and without Him was not anything made that was made.'—ST. JOHN I. 3.

'Ah, helpless wretch! condemned to dwell
For ever in my native shell.'—COWPER.

'HERE is Thorne; perhaps he can tell us. Luke, what is the price of a Paper Nautilus shell?' asked Edward, a day or two after his accident with Poppy's box.

As he spoke, he and Robert were engaged in counting the contents of their money-boxes, which were standing open on the table before them, with a large pile of coppers and a very small pile of silver by the side.

'You can get a very good one for two pounds or two pounds ten.'

The boys' faces fell.

'And we have five shillings and sevenpence between us, and only threepence a week each coming in, and there are just six weeks to Christmas—eight and sevenpence; and that old Argonaut costs two pounds at the least,' said Robert.

'We shall have our Christmas money from the grand-pater taken—I knew we should. He always gives us a sovereign each, and that is every penny we get at Christmas, so we sha'n't be able to give any presents. It's a shame!—for, after all, it was an accident. I wish there weren't such an animal as an Argonaut. There is a Nautilus; there was no occasion to have a Paper Nautilus as well,' said Edward in a grumbling voice.

'I wish there weren't such an animal as a girl; there are boys—there was no need to have made girls as well. Why couldn't Poppy have been a boy?' said Robert in the same tone.

'When you have quite finished your criticisms on the Divine economy, I have a suggestion to make,' said Luke in a quiet, satirical tone.

'A fine one, I daresay, when we have heard it. Perhaps a suggestion that we sell all our rabbits,' said Robert.

'Or that we ask father to give us the money he generally spends on our Christmas presents. Your suggestion is sure to be one we shall fall into with pleasure,' said Edward; for both boys were out of temper.

'I flatter myself it is one you'll jump at, though not so excellent an one as either of your own.'

'Well, let us have it. We may as well hear it; there is no occasion to adopt it,' said Robert.

'Not the slightest. It was merely this: I was going to offer to contribute two pounds towards the shell. I want to give you boys a Christmas-box, and if you don't mind having it so long before, here it is.' And as Luke spoke he pushed two sovereigns towards the little pile of silver.

For a minute there was a dead silence. The boys were too much astonished to speak, and Luke rose to leave the room, when Robert seized his hand, and, shaking it vigorously, exclaimed :

'You are a good fellow, and no mistake, Thorne ! We are awfully obliged to you.'

'I should think we were ; it is such a handsome present. The only thing is, I am afraid father won't let us accept it,' added Edward.

'I had thought of that; but, if I were you, I should send to Sowerby for a Paper Nautilus at once. Tell him it must not exceed two pounds five—you can get a beauty for that, I know. Send him a postal order, and then when the shell arrives, if Mr. Merton asks any questions, you can say you had a present of two pounds; you need not say from whom, unless he presses the question.'

This seemed so good a plan that the boys went off to the post-office for a postal order at once, and then wrote to Sowerby to request him to send them a Paper Nautilus by return of post, while Luke went to give Poppy another lesson.

'Now, Poppy, do you remember the meaning of Pteropoda ?' began Luke.

'Wing-footed. Now I am sure you thought I had forgotten, but I had not, you see.'

'Quite right. It is with the *Pteropoda*, the next class, we have to do to-day; the Pteropods are a very small class, containing only three families, one of which has no shell. They are to be found in all seas from Pole to Pole, but they avoid land, and are met with in deep seas—calm or rough, it matters not, but always far from shore. They are nocturnal, generally—or at least crepuscular—in their habits.'|

'Say they come out at twilight, please. I don't allow such words as crepuscular.'

'They are said by Mr. Forbes to be Neptune's butterflies, because they lead such a sportive life, swimming about with their fins, which project from their heads, on the surface of a moonlit sea, or sometimes sporting on the sunny surface of a calm sea, so that for miles they discolour the water. And you will readily believe how numerous they are, when I tell you that one species is the principal food of the Greenland whale, and of sea-birds.'

'What do they live on themselves?'

'On any smaller and weaker Molluscs which come in their way, or on the young of other fish. In appearance they are very like the fry of snails; they have no true foot—or, at any rate, it is very small; they can hear, and probably smell; but they have very rudimentary eyes and tentacles. They have a liver, a gizard, a heart, and an organ by which they breathe. The shell, when they possess one, is transparent and glassy; it is univalve, but generally consists of two united plates, with an opening in front for the head; sometimes it is conical, or coiled up spirally. These shells are rarely found ashore, but are brought up by dredging from the weed at the bottom of the sea. The first family is called *Hyaleidæ*, from a Greek word meaning glass. The shell of the *Hyalea* is globular in shape, translucent, glassy; the animal is also globular, with two flaps, or wings, which project from the side. There are nineteen species of these curious little shells, which are chiefly found in the Atlantic and Mediterranean; one species is called Venus' Chariot. The genus *Cleodora*, or *Clio*—for conchologists have agreed to differ on this point—are little pellucid pyramidal shells, with a triangular aperture at the base of the pyramid; they come from the Atlantic and Indian Oceans, where they may be seen in myriads on calm nights; they look like chips of fine glass, through which the organs of the animal can be distinctly seen. One species, *Cuspidata*, is luminous, and shows a spark of pale blue light through its translucent shell; it is found in the Pacific Ocean. One very singular genus I must not forget to mention—*Cymbula*. You have one specimen, Poppy, which I have heard you call Cinderella's shoe; it is a small, transparent, horny shell, in shape very like a pointed slipper, only large enough for a fairy's foot.'

'Oh, yes, I remember it well. It is a beautiful little shell; but it hardly looks like a shell at all.'

'No, it is not testaceous. There are only three species, found in the Atlantic and Indian Oceans and in the Mediterranean. The second family of the Pteropoda is the *Limacinidæ*, or Snail-like shells; they are minute, glassy, spiral shells, and left-handed or sinistral, by which they may be known from the fry of Gasteropods. One species of the genus *Limacina* is found on our coasts, but it is not bigger than a pin's head; yet, small as it is, the animal can retire into it and close the opening with a thin operculum. Some species resemble a miniature Argonauta; a few are turreted. The last family, the *Chidæ*, have neither mantle nor shell, so they don't come under our notice. Now we have arrived at the *Brachiopoda.*'

'I do hope they are bivalves; I am longing to get to the bivalves,' said Poppy.

'Yes, they are; but they are peculiar. Their shells are always equal-sided, but never equivalve, and are often united by a hinge; they are symmetrical and like antique lamps, so they used formerly to go by the name of Lamp Shells; and the hole in the upper valve which admits the passage of a tentacle, by which the animal anchors itself to sea-weed, answers to the hole by which the wick passes into a lamp. The valves are dorsal and ventral; the latter is usually the larger, and has a beak which is perforated for the tentacle; they are fastened by a perfect hinge, so that they cannot be separated without injury; they are opened and closed by some very complicated muscles, and the tentacle or pedicel is also attached to the beak by a pair of muscles; these muscles leave marked impressions on the valves. The inside of the valves is lined with the two mantle lobes, the mantle in the case of the Brachiopoda having two functions to perform: not only has it to secrete the shell, but also it possesses veins, by means of which the animal breathes. The animals themselves have no foot, like other Molluscs, though the stalk by which most of them anchor themselves may in some measure answer to that organ. They have two hearts, but no breathing

organ, the mantle performing that function for them.
They take their name from two long arms near their
mouth, whose use it is to create currents to bring them
food; and the manner in which these arms are folded
determines the different genera.'

' Aren't most of them fossil ? '

' There are over a thousand extinct species known, and
only about seventy recent species, so I suppose the
Brachiopods may be said to have had their day; but
yet they are found in all climates, in tropical and polar
seas,. and at all depths, from the shore pool to the
deepest ocean beds reached by dredging. Deep seas
seem to suit them best, however; so probably many more
species will be discovered in course of time. They are
all marine, and are very often found hanging by their
byssus to other shells, to rocks, or to branches of corals.
When quite young, they are free and swim about where
they will, but as they grow older they settle down on
some spot which suits them, and adhere by their byssus
to that. They rejoice in some very long names, so you
must not be angry with me, as I was not godfather to
any of them. The first family is the *Terebratulidæ*, or
Lamp Shells.'

' I hope there are not many families with such long
names as that.'

' There are eight; but some you have heard of before,
the Spirifers, for instance. However, I don't mean to
worry you with more than the Lamp Shells to-day.
Terebratula is the first genus; it means perforated. All
the family live in very deep seas, and fix themselves by
their wick or pedicel to each other or to some object.

Most of the shells are dull brown, but delicate and beautifully grooved, toothed at the edge, so that one valve fits exactly into the other.   The genus *Thecidium* resembles a small pouch, so-called from a Greek word meaning the same : the other genera vary little in name, and I think the general description I have given of the family will suffice,' said Luke, for Poppy was looking pale and tired.

'Thank you.   Do you know, Luke, it is nearly a year since I had my shells, and since *Gloria maris* was lost ? I have added nearly thirty new species to the collection since then ; but those thirty don't make up for the loss of *Gloria maris*, do they ?'

'No, indeed they don't.   I wonder if we shall ever solve that mystery ; it is so strange that we have not the slightest clue to it.'

'I wish the boys hadn't broken Argonauta ; it would have been something to have added that within the year.'

'So it would ; but I don't think you need be discouraged, Poppy.   See how much you have learnt.   If it were not for the loss of *Gloria maris*, I should say you had done splendidly.'

And a day or two later, when the Paper Nautilus arrived, and the boys placed the box in her hands for her to unpack, Poppy, as she drew the delicate white shell from its bed of cotton-wool, was inclined to agree with Luke.   Her delight was great, and she sent for all the family to come and admire her new treasure.

'Look, father, what a lovely Paper Nautilus the boys have given me ; isn't it a beauty ?'

L 2

'It is indeed; but how did you manage to get it, boys? It must have cost two pounds at the very least,' said Mr. Merton.

'It was two pounds five. It is a much better one than the one Graham sent you, Poppy,' said Edward.

'I should just think it was. It is lucky for you. Edward broke that,' said Robert.

'I can't see that quite, especially as the other was broken so successfully that we had none of us any opportunity of judging what it was like. But where did you get two pounds five from?' said Mr. Merton.

'We had five shillings in our money-box, and we had a present of a sovereign each a few days ago.'

'From whom?' said Mr. Merton, with a slight frown, and looking sharply at his wife.

'We half promised not to tell; must we say, father?'

'I can guess. It was Luke, I am sure. Luke, why did you do it?' said Poppy.

'I wanted to give the boys a Christmas present; and I wanted you to have an Argonauta; that was why. I hope you are not vexed, sir,' with an apologetic glance at Mr. Merton, who was looking very grave.

'Oh, no; I am sure father does not mind; he likes me to have everything I wish for, and I did so wish for a Paper Nautilus,' said Poppy.

'Well, I suppose I must not say anything, then. But I hope you boys have thanked Luke for such a handsome present; it is a great deal more than you deserved.'

'Oh, yes, they have. And now, Poppy, I want to talk to you about the Brachiopods; though, as most of the remaining genera are fossil, we shall soon finish with them, and get on to the Conchifera. The Spirifers are only known in the fossil state; they are used as medicine in China, where they abound. The next two families are extinct, or at least nearly so, as only one or two living species, with very long names, exist; but there are five living species of *Crania* found on the coasts of Scotland and Ireland and in the Indian Ocean. The shell is somewhat square, the upper valve like a limpet shell, the lower flat; there is no hinge, but the lower valve is attached to the animal, and bears distinctly marked muscular impressions. The animal has two short spiral arms, curved inwards, and fringed with long, stiff white fringes, which can protrude slightly beyond the shell. The animal of *Anomaila*, is orange-coloured; it is gregarious, and found on rocks and stones in deep water. The *Discina* possess seven living species, found in the northern seas, and also off the coasts of Peru, Chili, and Panama. The shell is horny, and disk-like in shape; the upper valve basin-shaped, the lower flat, with a sunk disk, which is perforated. The interior of the shell is polished, and when wet the entire shell is flexible. The animal is transparent, and has two short ciliated arms?'

'What does ciliated mean?'

'Fringed; it is derived from *cilium*, an eye-lash. The last of the Brachiopods is the family of *Lingulidæ*; of these there are seven living species of the genus *Lingula*, which means a little tongue. The valves of these shells, which are tongue-like in shape, are nearly equal, and have no hinge. They are thin, and often horny, and are covered with a horny epidermis. They are attached by a thick fleshy pedicel, for the animal sticks closely to its shell, and is even united to the epidermis. The margins of the mantle-lobes are fringed all round, and the pedicel is often nine inches long. The shell is flexible, and greenish in colour. In the Philippine Islands they are found plentifully at low water in the sand, and are used by the inhabitants as food. On the whole, not very much is known about the Lingula. If you like to make a contribution to science, you can obtain some living specimens and watch them. Are you tired ? Because, if not, we will go on to the *Conchifera.*'

'Not in the least. I have been longing to get to them, because I don't call the Brachiopods real *bonâ fide* bivalves, after all ; they are unsatisfactory creatures. I don't care for them.'

'Neither fish, flesh, nor good red herring, eh, Poppy ? Perhaps I should have left them to the last, but Woodward, who is my text-book, places them between the univalves and bivalves proper, or Conchifera. These last are certainly the more important, for they are more abundant individually than the univalves. They are all aquatic, and nearly all marine ; they occur in every climate and on all coasts. Some lie on one side, fixed to one spot, and completely visible, like the oyster. Some live in sand and mud, quite hidden from view. Some, like the mussel, remain visible, fixed to one spot by a byssus ; but the greater number live bolt upright, resting on the edges of their shells. Some bore holes for themselves in wood ; and some lie hidden in other shells, or in corals, or in holes in rocks. They live on slime and Infusoria, which they obtain by filtering water through their gills; not upon prey caught between their valves. They help to purify water by this means, as you would easily see, if you were to place some bivalves in water coloured with indigo; for in a short time they would have taken up all the indigo in their filters, and the water would be quite clear. The borers are sometimes called "stone-eaters," for they are obliged sometimes to swallow the wood or stone they are boring through, though they receive no nourishment from it. The shell consists of two parts, or valves bound together by an elastic ligament, and jointed by a hinge, one side of which locks firmly into the other. The shell opens by means of the ligament spontaneously, but it is closed by powerful muscles. Some bivalves live with their shells open, and are called "gapers," others live with closed shells. The shell itself consists of two layers, the outer one consisting of prismatic cells filled with carbonate of lime; the inner has no cells, but is laminated—that is, it consists of plates, or *laminœ*, lying one above the other. The valves are both attached to the animal by muscles fastened to the inner side, and also by the epidermis, which covers the exterior of the valves, and is connected with the mantle. This epidermis ends sometimes in silky threads or hairs, sometimes it is horny.'

'And the animal itself, what is that like, I wonder?'

'Well, I hardly know how to describe such non-descript creatures; moreover, they vary very much.

Some have a sort of foot, or at least a muscular appendage, by means of which they move about. This varies in form exceedingly: sometimes it is like a hook, sometimes like a worm or a tongue, always adapted to the use the animal requires it for, whether to creep, or bore, or jump. Other stationary species have no real foot, only a byssus, by which they moor themselves to some object. They have a mouth, but it is a strange mouth, for it has no jaws, but it is armed with tentacles, and this strange mouth is near the back of the animal. Some of the Conchifera have eyes, and when they have, these are always placed on the edge of the mantle, and are of a high organisation. The Pectens have beautiful emerald eyes. They all have a heart, though their blood is colourless. They have also a liver, and most of them a gizzard also, and generally two pairs of gills; these are flat membranes attached to the mantle, and I need not add by means of these the animal breathes. In the Pectens and some other families these gills are cut up into fringes. The gills have a great deal to do: they create currents; they catch the minute particles of animal or vegetable matter on which the animal feeds, and push them on towards the mouth; and in some genera they receive the eggs, and keep them until they are hatched; so you see they are very important organs in the bivalve's economy. And talking of important, I forgot to say that the bivalves are far more important to man than all the other Molluscs put together, because we use them so largely as food; and also we obtain pearls from some of them, so they are exceedingly valuable creatures.'

'Do stop and tell me how pearls are produced.'

'Well, in the first place, they are only found in nacreous shells. The best come from the Oriental pearl mussel, and some from *Unio margaritiferus*, a British river mussel. They are produced by particles of sand or carbonate of lime getting between the animal and its shell; these particles irritate the animal, and it deposits a coating of nacre round the foreign particle: this makes what we call pearls. The Chinese produce them artificially by introducing little pieces of mother-of-pearl into the shell while the animal is alive, and when it is coated with nacre withdrawing it; for this nacre is always more brilliant than that which lines the shell. Round pearls, which are the most valuable, can only be formed in the soft parts of the animal. In shells which are not nacreous this same process takes place, but the result is not a pearl, but only a little prominence of shelly matter the same colour as the lining of the shell in which they are found. But to return to the Conchifera. They are divided first of all into two sections: the *Asiphonida*, in which the animals have no breathing siphons; and the *Siphonida*, the animals of which are provided with siphons; and these sections are subdivided into twenty-one families.'

'What are the rules by which they are divided?'

'Various marks guide us: for instance, the form of the foot; the manner in which the mantle-lobes are joined; the structure of the gills and of the shell; the habits of the animal, whether it prefers fresh or salt water; the equality or inequality of the valves; the way in which the hinge is toothed; whether the ligament which joins the valves is external or internal: these are all characteristic of the different families. In the burrowing shells the foot is strong and stout; in the mussel and pearl oyster and in others which spin a byssus it is grooved and shaped like a finger; in others it is deeply cut, and can be expanded like the foot of a snail; in the *Pholades*, or borers, it is very large, and quite fills up the front aperture of the valves; in the Ship Worm, *Teredo*, it is smaller, but the edges of the mantle form a collar round it.'

'Doesn't the shape of the shell matter in classification?'

'Oh, yes; whether the valves are regular or irregular matters very much. The valves are always hollow, though some are spiral, and then they resemble spiral univalves; in this case the left valve is like the ordinary univalve, the right valve is twisted the left-handed way, like a sinistral univalve. In the bivalves the apex or point from which the valve begins to grow is called the *umbo*, or beak, in the plural *umbones*. Sometimes the umbones are curved, as in *Venus*; sometimes straight, as in the Pectens; and sometimes they are spiral. The shells are often ornamented with ridges or ribs, which radiate from the umbones to the margin. I forgot to say that the position and number of muscular impressions is another characteristic of different families. I seem to be shooting out my information in a very hap-hazard fashion, Poppy; but I thought I would make these general observations on the Conchifera to-day, and then we can take the families regularly every day, if possible, for I should like to finish them before

Christmas. I don't think I told you that the tentacles which fringe the mantle as well as those with which the mouth is provided act as feelers.'

'No, I don't think you did. There is one question I wanted to ask you. Have the bivalves any ears?'

'They have organs of hearing, at any rate, though very rudimentary: two round capsules containing a little ball of carbonate of lime swimming in a clear fluid. I am afraid I must stop here, Poppy, for I have to go and inquire for a sick man for your father before tea,' said Luke, reluctantly closing his lesson.

CHAPTER X.

MR. DOBSON'S NEW THEORY.

'Every creature of God is good.'—1 TIMOTHY IV. 4.

'The Argonauts in blind amaze
Tossing about on Neptune's restless waves.'—*Endymion.*

THE shell lessons went on regularly, and as nothing
of any moment happened during the next few weeks
we must record them, at the risk of being tedious, for,
like Luke, we are anxious to get to the end of the
Conchifera. So was Mr. Merton, for he had begun to
suspect that Mrs. Merton, who had long ago discovered
Luke's secret, though she had only just ventured to
confide it to her husband, was right; and, acting on her
suggestion, he generally contrived to be present during
the shell-hour, as Poppy called it.

'The first family is the *Ostreidæ*, or Oyster family.
About the Oysters themselves, and about the Pectens,
I have already told you something I think, Poppy; but
there are several other genera. · The family characteristics are these: the animal is marine; it has a small
foot, spinning a byssus; the mantle is open and fringed;

the gills are large and crescent-shaped; the shell is irregular, the valves unequal, the umbones straight, the epidermis thin, the ligament internal. The first genus is the Oyster. There are sixty living species, and 200 fossil; one of these latter, found on the Tagus, is two feet long. By the way, the length of a bivalve is measured across from side to side, its breadth from the umbones to the margin.'

'Are all the sixty living species edible?'

'Oh, no; *edulis* is the edible oyster, but abroad many other species are eaten. One sub-genus, called *Gryphœa*, is very peculiar; the beak of the lower valve is produced and curved. There are thirty British species, all fossil. The next genus, *Anomia*, is not edible, but is often found attached to oysters and other shells, and can't be taken off without destroying the animal. It frequently takes the form of the object to which it is attached; it is phosphorescent. The shell varies very much; it is slightly nacreous inside and translucent; the valves are unequal, hence the generic name, for *anomios* is the Greek for unequal. The Window Shells, or *Placuna*, are nearly related to Anomia. There are only four species; they come from Asia and Australia. In China they are used for lanterns and windows, for they are translucent. They are nearly equivalve, thin, and very much compressed, and are made entirely of sub-nacreous plates, which are easily separated. Little is known of the animal, but as the valves when closed almost touch, it must be very flat. The Greek name means a thin plate. Now we come to the pretty Pectens, about which you have already heard a good deal, and I believe you have seven out of our nine British species.'

'Aren't the Pectens sometimes called quins, as well as scallops?'

'Yes; one species, *Opercularis*, is called the Quin, and, like the Scallop, is considered a great delicacy, and is largely eaten in Ireland. These shells are generally ornamented with ribs. The umbones are eared; the hinge margins are straight; the shell regular, found resting on the right valve. The animal has a finger-like foot, which spins a byssus when young. The mantle is open, and has its double margins fringed: the inner one is called the "curtain," and below it are a row of black eyes. The Pectens are found everywhere; and are much used in this country, particularly on the south coast, where they abound, as food. There are 120 species. The *Limas*, or Files, are much less numerous. There are only twenty species. The shell is always white; but in one species at least the animal makes up for the want of colour in the shell: it is pale crimson, with an orange mantle, and is one of the most beautiful Molluscs known. Like the Pecten, it can swim quickly by opening and closing its valves. It sometimes spins a byssus, sometimes it is free, and some species, when they come to maturity, make for themselves a burrow by spinning sand, shells, and bits of coral together. This burrow is closed at each end, and is a great deal longer than the shell.'

'Aren't the Limas those one-sided shells?' asked Poppy.

'They are obliquely oval, scientifically speaking; but

perhaps one-sided expresses their shape, to an unscientific mind at any rate. They are equivalve, gaping, sometimes ribbed, sometimes smooth; the umbones are apart and eared. The animal has a finger-like, grooved foot, equal gills on each side, mantle-margins separate, the inner curtain fringed with long threads, which, if cut off, live for hours, wriggling about like worms. There are twenty living species, the largest of which is found on the coast of Norway. Some are rare; three are found on our coast, the beautiful Hians, which I described to you, among them. They are all covered with a horny, brown epidermis.'

'What are you going to get?' interrupted Poppy, as Luke moved towards one of her cabinets.

'Only your thorny oysters, that you may admire them while I tell you the little there is left to tell. Certainly *Spondylus* is one of the most beautiful genera of bivalves, in colour if not in shape. Look at these reds and pinks and yellows. Now notice, Poppy, the under valve is always the most thorny and the least brilliant, probably because the animal rests on that valve. The inner layer of the shell is always distinct from the outer, and in fossil specimens this layer is absent. The shell is irregular, ribbed, and spiny, the beaks eared, the lower valve with a broad triangular boss, by which it is attached to rocks or corals. The animal is very like Pecten. It lives in very deep seas, on corals and rocks. It is sometimes found on anchors or other iron objects which have been under water for a long time. We have no British species. They come mostly from the Indies, America, and the Mediterranean. The last genus is *Plicatula*, which means plaited, and is so named because the valves are sometimes plaited. These shells come from the West Indies and the Philippines, and cannot be separated without breaking the valves, which are firmly locked together with grooved teeth. Now we come to the second family, the Wing Shells, or *Aviculidæ*, which, being very oblique, you probably call one-sided or crooked.'

'I call them very quaint, and I also call them Pearl Oysters; so you see I know rather more than you give me credit for.'

'So you do, for you are right; one species is called the Pearl Oyster; but we shall come to that presently. First let me tell you the family characteristics. These are, pearly lining to the shell, which is inequivalve and very oblique, the hinge-line is very long and straight, the beaks eared, the posterior ear wing-like. The animal has free mantle-lobes with fringed margins, a small foot, which spins a byssus, by which the shell is attached to some object. The genera are all tropical. All northern species are fossil and very numerous. The first genus is called *Avicula*, which means a little bird. Several beautiful species come from the Indian Ocean, Brazil, and the Mediterranean. The valves are wing-shaped, the interior pearly in the centre, which is sometimes surrounded by a black border, and the epidermis hangs in a fringe round the margin. The animal is shaped like the shell, the byssus is large, and passes through a notch. Your Pearl Oyster is a sub-genus, called *Meleagrina*, and is less one-sided or oblique than Avicula; the valves, too, are nearly equal, and flatter;

the shells are lined with mother-of-pearl, which is imported in large quantities into Europe for ornamental purposes from Ceylon and Madagascar, where the pearl oysters are found.'

'But, Luke, is it only mother-of-pearl which is found in the pearl oysters?'

'No; real pearls are found there. I was coming to them; if you remember, they are only lumps or excrescences formed by the introduction of some foreign matter, or a diseased egg, round which the most brilliant nacre coats itself. These are real Oriental pearls, and as you know, very valuable. Perhaps the quaintest of all the Aviculæ is the Hammer Oyster, from China and Australia, which, as it grows old, grows like a hammer in shape; but the form varies very much, so that two are rarely found alike. Consequently, some, quainter than others, are much run after by collectors, not so much for their beauty as for their quaintness; but the interior is always lined with brilliant nacre. I will omit three or four fossil genera, and go on to the *Pinnas*, or wings, though I have already told you something about them. The shell is wedge-shaped, equivalve, gaping, the hinge straight; sometimes the shell grows to two feet in length; it is always thin and brittle, when young it is translucent; it is only lined half-way with nacre, and this lining is thin. The animal spins a very powerful byssus, by which it moors itself to the sand, with its beaks plunged in, and its knife-like, gaping extremities sticking out. The Mussels, which come next, I told you about in my lecture; so I pass them over, and go on to the *Arcadæ*. These are regular,

M

equivalve shells, covered with a strong epidermis; the hinge is toothed with comb-like teeth; the mantle is open, the foot large, grooved, and bent, the gills oblique.'

'Why are they called Arks?'

'They are supposed, particularly Noah's Ark, which is the type of the genus *Arca*, to be like an ark, or a chest, in shape; but I confess the resemblance is not very striking, though the shape is somewhat remarkable. Some species have closed valves, and then the left valve is larger than the right. Some have a velvety epidermis, ending in a deep fringe. Some have a horny byssus, and the hole through which it passes is very large; these are called Bysso-Arks. They live in holes, or bury themselves under stones at low water, attaching themselves to corals or rocks by their byssus; they often get very much distorted. The Arks abound most in warm seas, but they are of world-wide distribution. In Australia, at Brisbane, they were formerly the chief food of the natives, and there are heaps of these shells twenty feet deep, covered with earth, and large trees growing on the top of them. Of the next genus, *Cucullea*, or a cowl, which very much resembles Arca in shape, we have only one species, which is found in the Indian Ocean; it is a deep brown colour, lined with brown, tinged with violet. The genus *Nucula*, which means a little net, has seventy species; some of which are British. The animal uses its foot for burrowing; this foot is large, and expands into a disk. The mouth and lips are very small; the interior of the shell is pearly; and that is all I have to say about the Arks; except that we have two pretty little British specimens of the genus *Leda*.'

'Doesn't my *Trigonia*, that lovely pearly shell of mine, lined inside with purple and gold, and pearly all over, belong to the Arks?'

'No; it belongs to the *Trigonidæ*. *Trigonos* is the Greek for three-angled, the shape of the shell, which is thick and entirely nacreous, as you say. When found in a fossil state in Portland stone, the Trigonias are called "horse-heads." The animal has a very strong muscular foot, and when caught has been known to leap overboard; they come from Australia, and are supposed to be migratory.'

'What are the Naïdes?'

'The River Mussels, or *Unionidæ*, is the family name; I am now coming to them, but I shall only describe the genus *Unio*; they are found in streams and ponds all over the world. One of them, *Unio margaritiferus* produces pearls. By the way, *Unio* means a pearl, and the name was given to the genus by Pliny. Formerly, round pearls, worth three or four pounds each, and as large as a pea, were found in these mussels in Scotland. The pearls used to be collected before harvest by the peasants in olden times.'

'Excuse me, Luke, but does every Unio, or River Mussel, contain a pearl?'

'Dear me, no, not one in a hundred; and of those that do, perhaps not one in a hundred is perfect. There is, as you know, a great difference in the quality of pearls; the shape affects the value, and so does the clearness.   The Swan Mussel, or *Anodon*, has large thin pearly valves, which, in France, are used for skimming milk.   They are a very prolific genus, and as many as 600,000 young shells have been counted in the gills of an adult.   This brings us to the end of the first section of the Conchifera; and as I think I am getting too like a hand-book, for the future, Poppy, you shall just ask me questions about the remaining families; you have specimens of nearly all of them.   Who can that be?   It is too late for visitors, and yet it was the hall-door bell,' said Luke, breaking off abruptly.

'Some one for father.   I hope you have not to go out this cold evening, father,' said Poppy.

'If you please, sir, Mr. Dobson wishes to speak to you.   I showed him into your study,' said a servant.

'Dobson? he has heard something of *Gloria maris*, then, you may depend,' said Luke excitedly.

'Perhaps he has found it.   Oh, father! do make haste and go and see!' said Poppy, sitting bolt upright in her eagerness.

'Take care, my child, lie down.   See to her, Luke,' said Mr. Merton, who was outwardly calm, but inwardly as excited as either of the young people.

He had not been gone long when the two boys burst into the drawing-room full of eagerness.

'I say, Poppy, here is a go!   Dobson is down here again about *Gloria maris*,' said Edward.

'He is closeted with father in his study,' said Robert.

'We could have told you that,' said Luke quietly.

'Yes, and Dobson thinks he has got a clue, and father is pooh-poohing it.'

'"Wildly improbable, most unlikely," is all father keeps saying. And Dobson answers, "The most unlikely things often happen."'

'But how do you know what father and Mr. Dobson are talking about? Were you in the room?' said Poppy.

'No, we—we listened; really, Poppy, we could not help it; we knew you would be dying to know all about it, so we crept to the door and peeped in through the keyhole.'

'It was very dishonourable, then; and I don't care to hear any more till father chooses to tell me,' said Poppy; whereupon the two boys, muttering something about what muffs girls were, but nevertheless feeling conscious that Poppy was right, took themselves off.

The interview in the study did not last half-an-hour, though it seemed more to Poppy and Luke, who were now joined by Mrs. Merton, whose curiosity was as great as theirs. At last Mr. Dobson was heard to take his departure, and Mr. Merton returned to the drawing-room, where he was met by a storm of inquiries as to the object of Mr. Dobson's visit.

'A wild-goose chase, in my opinion, a mere wild-goose chase,' said Mr. Merton, who looked annoyed and disappointed.

'Has he heard anything of the shell?' demanded Mrs. Merton.

'Did you know a housemaid of ours had gone to

live with Dobson as general servant?' said Mr. Merton, instead of answering his wife's question.

'Did I know it? No; why, yes, though, of course; now I come to remember, it was a Mrs. Dobson who wrote for her character, but I never supposed she had any connection with our Mr. Dobson; that accounts for the girl's leaving us; she was never settled here after the Dobsons were here in the summer. How very stupid of me not to have realised where she had gone till this moment! I see it all now; evidently Mr. Dobson wished the girl to leave us, for I did not want to part with her at all; but what about her?'

'Why, Dobson has got out of her that I walk in my sleep occasionally; and as you were out on the Saturday night during which the shell might have been stolen— for it might have been taken on the Sunday night when you were at home—he has jumped at the conclusion that I did something with *Gloria maris* in my sleep.'

'Well, it is just probable that he may be right,' said Mrs. Merton thoughtfully.

'It is most improbable, wildly improbable, as I told him; what on earth should I have done with it?' said Mr. Merton irritably.

'Perhaps put it into some safer place,' suggested Mrs. Merton.

'Pshaw! My dear, you are as bad as Dobson; that is exactly what he said. If he has no better suggestions than that to make, he had better keep in London, and not come rushing down here for such nonsense; and I was very much inclined to tell him so.'

The truth was, Mr. Merton was very touchy about his somnambulism; few things annoyed him more than to have it mentioned; and to have it suggested that he had made away with the shell, or at least hidden it, so that it was practically lost, annoyed him exceedingly. The fact that the shell was lost was in itself sufficiently vexatious, particularly when Mr. Merton knew that it imperilled Poppy's fortune; for even if she continued to add to the collection till she came of age, it would deteriorate in value by the loss of so valuable a shell as *Gloria maris*, and it was a question whether by the terms of the will she would not forfeit all but that legacy of 500*l*. unless the Glory of the Sea were recovered. This knowledge Mr. Merton had to keep to himself, and the consequence was the loss of the shell worried him far more than it did any of the others, for he only knew what a very important matter it was. And although his solicitor assured him he felt sure the disappearance of the gem of the collection would not cause Poppy to forfeit her fortune, still he admitted there was a doubt; and that doubt was enough to make her father exceedingly uncomfortable, when it was suggested he had mislaid the shell.

'Well, at any rate, Dobson's suggestion is worth considering. There is no harm in looking again for the shell.'

'No harm, and no good; the house has been searched from attic to basement over and over again; but if you choose to institute another search, pray do so,' said Mr. Merton, leaving the room to hide his annoyance.

Mrs. Merton did choose to look again; so the next day another thorough search in cupboards, and drawers, and various likely and unlikely places was made; but all in vain; no *Gloria maris* was found, and once again the quest was given up as fruitless.

CHAPTER XI.

SHIPWORMS, VENUS SHELLS, AND KELLIAS.

'And God saw everything that He had made, and behold it was very good.'—GEN. I. 31.

'Here subterranean works and cities see.'—POPE.

'I NEVER expect to see *Gloria maris* again. I have quite given it up, and I think I am resigned to it,' said Poppy to Luke when he came to renew his lesson the next day.

'I don't think we shall ever see it again; it is a thousand pities, but I suppose it can't be helped. We won't talk of it any more. Now, Poppy, what do you wish me to begin with to-day? You know all the remaining Conchifera are those which breathe through a siphon, and there are fourteen families of them.'

'I want you to tell me about the Ship Worms first, please; those dreadful creatures that make holes in ships.'

'The *Teredo;* they belong to the *Pholadidœ,* or borers. You are quite right, they are dreadful things. They threatened to destroy some of the towns in Holland in the last century by boring through the piles. They always bore in the direction of the grain of the wood, and are very careful never to invade each other's burrows, though they may be close together and very winding; though whether they are guided by hearing in this caution, or whether the wood itself yields, is not certain. Soft wood is destroyed very quickly by it, and even oak and teak suffer from its ravages. The animal is like a worm; it is sometimes a foot, sometimes two feet and a half, long. The lobes of the mantle are united, but they open in front to admit of the passage of the foot, which is like a sucker. The shell is globular and attached to the animal, which also lines its burrow with a thin layer of shelly matter.'

'What does it bore with, its foot?'

'Yes; this is studded with particles of silica, which help it; but some naturalists think it bores with the edges of its little shell, which are very sharp and have a curved tooth under each boss. To avoid the ravages of these mischievous creatures, our ships are obliged to be copper-bottomed, if going a long voyage. And yet they do some good to make up for their evil habits; they bore through wreckage which might otherwise be dangerous, and cause it to break up and fall to pieces. The Giant Teredo makes a burrow a yard long and two inches in diameter at its widest part, so you may imagine what a terror sailors have of it. There is another species, *Corniformis*, which makes very tortuous burrows in the shells of tropical fruits, cocoa-nuts, for instance, and palm-trees. The *Teredina*, when it is full grown, cements its valves to its burrow, and there spends the rest of its days.'

'Now tell me about the *Pholas* itself. I have some shells; they are a long oval, and delicate, almost transparent, pure white, with rows of long prickles.'

'Yes, most of the Pholas are white; they are thin, and gape at both ends; from one end the breathing tubes issue, from the other the thick powerful foot which bores through stone and rock, according to some naturalists, who maintain that the foot is armed with rasping instruments of great power, and that by degrees this foot wears away the rock or stone which the water has softened. Other naturalists think the shells, which, though brittle, are exceedingly hard and armed in front with rasps, perform the office. I believe the latter to be undoubtedly the true theory, for they can perforate any substance softer than their own valves; a third theory suggests that the animal has the power of ejecting some acid which wears away the stone. The English name for the Pholas is the piddock; on the Devonshire coast the common piddock is much used for bait. Its foot is white and translucent, like a piece of ice; it is not eaten in this country, but some large species found in the Mediterranean are used for food. Pliny first mentioned that the animal is phosphorescent, and it is the only testaceous Mollusc which is. It is said to illuminate the mouth of the person eating it, and the fresher it is, the greater its luminous power; it can throw off some of this luminous membrane into the sea, so that at night the currents it makes and whatever it touches shine brilliantly.'

'It is a much nicer animal than Teredo.'

'I think it is; it has the property of throwing out

water when irritated; but as this is luminous, perhaps you would not quarrel with it on that account. By the way, I must not forget to tell you that there are Pholas-hunters in places where the piddocks abound and these men's clothes are entirely covered with a brilliant white, owing to a kind of cement which flies out of the rocks as they break into them with their pickaxes in search of the Pholades, and covers them, so that they look as if dressed in white. Did I tell you the name Pholas is derived from *pholeo*, to bore? The borers lead us naturally to the burrowers, so if you have no objection, Poppy, we will take the *Gastrochenidæ*, or burrowers in mud and stone, next.'

'I object to the name very much; what does it mean?'

'Gaping ventrally. All the family have valves which, though closed behind, gape widely in front. These animals are often gregarious, and live in large colonies near low-water mark. They are very fond of their burrows, and it is a difficult matter to get them out of their homes. The shells are thin and equivalve, not toothed, but the valves joined by a ligament. The *Gastrochena* itself is a small shell, seldom more than half an inch long, wedge-shaped, gaping widely in front. It penetrates limestone and other shells, making regular holes half an inch in diameter and two inches long. In burrowing in oyster shells, it often passes through the shell into the ground below, and makes a sort of flask with anything it finds, and fixes the neck of this into the oyster shell, taking up its abode in the globe. As many as a dozen have been found in one oyster shell. It is a native of Great Britain, but is also found in India, America, and the Mediterranean. The genus *Clavagella*, which is rare and found in coral chiefly, makes fringes, sometimes as many as six to its tube. Its shell is oblong, with flat valves, the left cemented to the burrow. The animal has a closed mantle, with a small opening for its tiny foot. One species spirts out water when irritated. We have no species here. The Pacific and the Mediterranean are its home. The Watering Pot shell belongs to this family. It is found in sand in tropical seas. The shell, which is small, is cemented to the lower end of a long shelly tube, the beak only visible. One end of this tube is closed with a perforated disk, the other is ornamented with frills or fringes, varying in number from one to eight, and resembling the spout of a watering-pot. It is a most curious shell, varying in length, tube included, from six inches to a foot. It is white, tinged with pale red or grey. There are only these three genera of burrowers.'

'Well, now, please, tell me about the Venuses.'

'*Veneridæ*, Poppy; I think I must insist on your learning Latin with the boys,' said Mr. Merton, who just then entered the room.

'I wish you would, sir; then I should not be made to define every word I use of Latin or Greek derivation. Well, Poppy, as you know the Veneridæ are remarkable for the beauty of their shapes and colours, and are found in all parts of the globe, but most abundantly in the tropics. Most of the species serve as food for man, and are found buried in the sand. The *Venus* has a

thick egg-shaped shell, toothed. There are no less than
176 species, some of which, as you know, are very
beautiful. One species, *Mercenaria*, was formerly used
as money by the North American Indians, who strung
fragments of it on leathern thongs. Other species are
ribbed, and many beautifully sculptured. The genus
Artemis, which you perhaps know is the Greek name
for Diana, has mostly white shells, nearly round, and
seldom so beautifully polished or coloured as *Venus;*
but, like many other beautiful creatures, the Veneridæ
are not so interesting as other less favoured Molluscs;
so choose another family.'

'Let me choose, Poppy. I should like to hear about
the *Lucinidæ*,' said Mr. Merton.

'Does your friend Aristotle, the king of naturalists,
mention them then, sir?'

'Not that I recollect.'

'Well, they are pretty shells, quite worthy of his and
our notice. They are found in most seas and at all
depths. The shells are orb-like, closed, and unattached,
dull and furrowed inside. The animals have one or
two siphons, a long, strap-shaped foot, and large, thick
gills; a small mouth. In *Lucina*, the foot is hollow
and often twice as long as the animal, but generally
folded back and hidden between the gills. There
are seventy species, none British, though some are
European.'

'Does not my pretty Basket shell belong to the
Lucinidæ?'

'*Corbis*, you mean. Yes, it does. There are only
two species; so you may think yourself lucky to possess

one, for they are rare. They come from India and the Pacific. They are thick, solid shells, furrowed and ridged so as to look like basket-work—hence their name. Another pretty little shell found on our own coasts is *Kellia*. It produces a very fine, delicate thread, by which it suspends itself from crevices of rocks or roots of sea-weed. These shells are small and thin, the valves closed, the margins smooth, and the beaks small; the hinges vary. The animals creep about or fix themselves by a byssus. They have been taken off the Irish coast in the stomachs of mullet.'

'Poor, pretty Kellias, what an untimely end!'

'Not so bad as the *Mactras*, for they are collected in Ireland to feed pigs, and if they escape that ignoble fate they become the food of star-fish and whelks. But, after all, if you must be eaten, it does not much matter what eats you, pigs, mullet, or star-fish.'

'Not much; but tell us about the Mactras, please, Luke.'

'They inhabit sandy shores in all parts of the world, though they prefer the tropics. They live in the sand just below the surface. Some species are rare and beautiful. A few are British. The word *Mactra* means a kneading-trough. The shell is oval, and may be known by the front hinge-tooth, which is shaped like the letter V, and locks into a cavity in the other valve. The shell is generally thin. The animal has a fringed mantle, united siphons, also fringed, and a large, tongue-shaped foot, which can be lengthened and moved about like a finger, and can also be used for jumping. *Gnathodon*, another genus of the *Mactridæ*, has only one living and one fossil species. The living species comes from New Orleans, where it is found in a lake and used as food. It is also found on the mud banks of the Gulf of Mexico in shoals about two or three inches deep in the mud; and inland for twenty miles, banks of dead shells, three or four feet thick, are found, and one road of six miles is made of these shells.'

'Do the *Tellens* belong to the Mactras?'

'No, they are a distinct family; but really Mactras and Tellens may be called first-cousins of the Mussels. The Tellens are often richly coloured and beautifully sculptured and elegantly shaped. They are found in all seas, buried beneath the surface in sand or mud. The shells are inequivalve, one being sometimes more convex than the other. Some valves, too, are more twisted than others, and the bands of colour also vary. The animal has the power of leaping, by compressing its foot and then suddenly extending it, closing its valves with a click which can be distinctly heard at the same time. We have ten native species, but the most beautiful are found only in the tropics. They bore into the sand, and are preyed upon by larger shell-fish. I think I mentioned *Psammobia*, the Sunset shell, which belongs to the same family, before.'

'Yes, you did; but you have never mentioned *Semele* or *Donax*; and I think they must belong to the *Tellenidæ?*'

'Yes, they do. Donax is the Wedge shell. It is shaped like a wedge, and was so named by Pliny. It is found in the Baltic, the Black Sea, and all tropical seas, buried in the sand below low-water mark. Some species are beautiful, though they are not remarkable for brilliancy of colour. They are covered with a pale horny epidermis; there are several British species. *Semele* is a small, oval, white shell, found on our coasts, and in Norway, the Mediterranean, and India. It has a large pointed tongue-shaped foot, with which it can creep over the sides of a boat if captured. Its home is in mud or sand. And now, Poppy, I believe I have mentioned every family except the Lantern Shells and some fossils.'

'Yes, I think you have, for I suppose the Heart Cockle belongs to the cockle family?'

'Oh, no, it does not. Thank you for mentioning it. *Isocardia*, or the Heart Cockle, belongs to the *Cyprinidœ*, a family rejoicing in some very poetical names: *Cyprina, Astarte, Circe, Isocardia*, etcetera. One half of these genera are extinct, and the remaining genera are much less abundant now than formerly, excepting *Circe*. They are regular oval equivalve shells, with a thick dark epidermis, and closed solid valves. The animals have a thick tongue-shaped foot. The shell of Isocardia is heart-shaped, the bosses spiral, and so peculiar as to make the genus unmistakable. There are five species, one of which is British. The Lantern Shells, or *Anatinidœ*, which means pertaining to a duck, are a large family containing ten genera. They are thin, nacreous inside, frequently iridescent outside; sometimes the exterior is rough, with chalky cells, and covered by an epidermis. The *Anatina*, or Lantern Shell itself, is delicate, rare, and brittle. Some species are very beautiful. It is oblong, thin, and translucent,

N

gaping at the thinner end; the hinge is spoon-shaped. The shell is found in India, New Zealand, and Western America. The genus *Pandora* contains pretty little oblong shells, pearly within; some of which are found on our southern coasts and in Jersey. They burrow in sand and mud.'

'Look here, Luke, what is this shell? I don't think you have mentioned it,' said Mr. Merton, who was amusing himself by pulling in and out some of the drawers of one of Poppy's cabinets.

'It is a *Chama*. I have forgotten the Chamas, though there are sixty species. They are found in tropical seas, chiefly among coral-reefs. They vary exceedingly both in shape and colour. They are sometimes found fixed to each other in masses; sometimes fixed to a rock, and so firmly fastened that it is difficult to remove them without breaking the shell, which consists of three layers, and is spiny. And with them, Poppy, I think I must close our lessons for the present, as I shall be very busy till Christmas. Perhaps after that your zeal may have increased so far as to lead you to care about the Tunicaries, which have only a tunic in place of a shell.'

'Perhaps it will, and perhaps by then *Gloria maris* will have turned up; I can't tell why, but I feel more hopeful since Mr. Dobson's last visit,' said Poppy.

Luke did not answer, nor did Mr. Merton, who was engaged in examining, for at least the hundredth time since the shell was lost, the secret drawer.

CHAPTER XII.

THE TUNICARIES.

'The rich and poor meet together: the Lord is the Maker of
them all.'—Prov. xxii. 2.

'The sea hath its pearls; the heaven hath its stars;
But my heart, my heart, my heart hath its love.'—Heine.

Luke Thorne returned to the Rectory after Christmas; but the lessons were not resumed, as he was
reading hard, and was to be ordained at Easter, when
it was arranged he should come back to King's Cliff as
Mr. Merton's curate. He was not to live at the Rectory
then, but in lodgings in the village. All this came to
pass, and somehow Luke contrived to see almost as
much of the Rectory people when installed in his new
'diggings' as he did when he lived at the Rectory, for a
day never passed without his dropping in for half an
hour.

Early in the summer Poppy went up to London with
her mother to see her doctor. She was away from home
nearly a month, and on the day of her return Mr.
Merton invited Luke to tea to welcome her back.

N 2

'I have had rather a mysterious letter from Mrs. Merton. She specially requests that I will order a fly to meet them, and that you and I and the boys remain at home to receive them. I don't know why, unless she objects to my driving on the box, for there would be no room inside with Poppy lying down.'

'How is Poppy? Does Mrs. Merton say there is any hope of her recovery?' asked Luke anxiously.

'I can't make out from her letters what the doctor's opinion is, she says so little; but I fear there is not much hope, or she would be more explicit. It is very sad, my poor little Poppy! Well, Thorne, you'll be here at five; they will arrive shortly after, and as Poppy also urges me not to meet them, I must fall in with their wishes.'

Luke acquiesced, and long before five on the day of their expected return he was up at the Rectory to welcome them. It was a hot June day, and tea was laid on the lawn in front of the house; and Mr. Merton, the two boys, and Luke were engaged in a game of tennis when wheels were heard in the drive. With one consent they threw down their rackets, and hastened to the hall door, arriving at the same time as the fly containing Mrs. Merton and Poppy.

'Look at Poppy! she is sitting up like mother!' exclaimed Edward.

'And she looks quite well!' said Robert.

'So she is!' said Poppy, springing out of the carriage as soon as it stopped, and rushing into her astonished father's arms.

'See, father, I am quite well! Aren't you glad? I

would not let mother tell you, because I wanted it to be a surprise.'

'My darling, my darling, thank God!' was all poor Mr. Merton could mutter, in a broken voice, as he held the tall, slim figure of his daughter in his arms.

'How tall you are, Poppy, and how thin!' exclaimed the boys.

'I am no taller than I was when I went away, but I am thinner, because I am all myself now. I have no horrid plaster-of-paris case. Is not it splendid? Luke, boys, aren't you glad? I shall be able to walk about like other people now.'

Luke was almost as overcome by the joy of Poppy's recovery as her father, and could only mumble something very indistinctly, as he shook both her hands; while Mrs. Merton was quietly crying for joy behind her veil, as she superintended the moving of the luggage into the house.

'Will you be able to play tennis, Poppy?'

'No, that is one of the things I am not to do. Riding and skating are the two other forbidden things; but as I neither ride nor skate, I sha'n't mind that; and perhaps next year I shall be allowed to play tennis. I may walk as much as I like, if I don't overtire myself; so I shall be able to go shell-hunting on my own account now, and I can help father in the parish. He'll have to keep two curates now instead of one.'

'Why didn't you tell us you were so much better, Poppy?'

'Because I wanted to surprise you all. I think pleasant surprises are such nice things; and I knew you would all be nearly as glad as I am—perhaps gladder, because you won't have to wait on me now.'

'We never minded that much,' said Luke.

And then Poppy insisted on making tea and waiting on her father, and was so happy that Mr. Merton, who was terribly afraid she should do too much, had not the heart to say anything to damp her joy, though his anxious face betrayed his fears, and led Mrs. Merton, who was more used to Poppy's convalescence, to reassure him.   But it was some time before he got used to seeing her run about the house and garden, and start off walking with her brothers; and for weeks after her return Mr. Merton lived in dread of seeing her do too much and being obliged to return to her sofa. As he said, the good news was so good he hardly dared to believe in it. But by degrees he too got used to it, and Poppy walked and drove like other people, and declared she had almost forgotten she had ever been an invalid, only that the pleasure of using her legs was so much greater than it could have been if she had never known what it was to be deprived of the use of them. As the summer went on she was able to go shell-hunting with Luke Thorne and the boys; and many were the happy hours they spent wading among rocks and pools at low water, armed with an iron rake, their hands covered with thick gloves, to protect them from the stings of Medusæ and the sharp spines and back-fins of sting-fish and sea-hedgehogs. Luke and the boys would lift up large stones, under which some prize was found lurking, or climb up rocks to search the ledges and crevices, while Poppy was content to hunt the pools and more accessible rocks. For Limpets and Chitons they were obliged to take a flat knife, called the spatula, the use of which Poppy always delegated to Luke, for she disliked hurting any of her prey, and the killing on their return always distressed her. Most of the Molluscs they found were killed by boiling, after which the animals were easily removed, for bivalves gape when the animal is dead; but the Chitons meet a crueller fate: they must be pressed, living, between two boards to preserve their shells properly. They found that Ormers and some other obstinate adherers can be removed from rocks by pouring warm water over them, and then giving them a sharp push sideways: mere force is of no use. Of course the spring-tides were the best time for these hunting excursions, because then the tide goes out farthest; and the highest spring-tides are always in September and March, at the equinox. Then it was often necessary to dig in the sand and mud for burying bivalves. But they soon found the chief thing was to look very closely in holes and crevices, under stones and among sea-weeds; by so doing they often found minute species, which, in a superficial search would be easily overlooked. Sometimes they carried home a basket of sea-weed and plunged it into a basin of fresh water, when the animals fell to the bottom. In this way they occasionally brought home some of the Tunicaries, which roused Poppy's curiosity, and induced her the next winter to ask Luke to tell her something about them.

'If I do, you'll be wanting an aquarium; for many of them are very beautiful, and I am sure you won't care to preserve them in spirits, though they retain a great deal of their beauty when so kept.'

'No, that I certainly sha'n't; but I sha'n't want to possess them at all. I have my shells; that is enough. But I may as well learn a little about the Tunicaries.'

'They inhabit all seas, so we often come across them in our shell hunts, and curious-looking objects they are; inside the outer tunic, which takes the place of the shell, is an inner tunic, corresponding to the mantle in other Molluscs; within this mantle is a third more delicate tunic, which acts as a breathing sac, at the bottom of which is the animal's mouth; the heart is near the posterior end of the body. There are some coloured spots near the openings of the mantle, which are supposed to be rudimentary eyes, and some capsules supposed to be ears. Some of them produce their young from eggs: these are larvæ, very like the tadpoles of frogs; they have oval bodies, black specks for eyes, and a long tail, which they use as a fin to swim about with. Then they fix themselves to rocks, or shells, or sea-weed, and the tail is absorbed. The *Tunicata* are divided by Huxley into three groups: (1) the Simple Ascidians, (2) the Social Ascidians, and (3) Compound Ascidians. The Simple Ascidians, are well described by Aristotle in his history of animals. They are sometimes solitary, sometimes gregarious, but always fixed, and they produce their young from eggs.'

'Please tell me why they are called Ascidians.'

'From the Greek word *askos*, a skin bottle, which they somewhat resemble in shape. They vary in length, at least, the *Ascidii*, or Sea Squirts, which are the first genus, do, from one to five or six inches. The tunic is pale and semi-transparent, through which gleams the inner crimson or orange tunic, sometimes marbled with white. The eye-spots are red or yellow. They are found in most seas, attached to rocks or shells or sea-weed. We have nineteen species. The Molgulas are rounder, and when taken in the dredge come up as a little ball of sand. There are three species only, found here and in Denmark. The Cynthias are found in the Mediterranean, sometimes on oysters or sea-weed, very often in great numbers, so that they are taken in bunches. They are considered a great delicacy, and are sold in the market at Cette. Some of the other Simple Ascidians are also largely eaten in Brazil and China, and in some parts of Italy.'

'By the way, I once had some served up on board an Italian steamer, and thought them exceedingly salt and nasty; but as I was suffering very much from sea-sickness, perhaps I was not a fair judge of their taste,' said Mr. Merton.

'If Poppy would care to try them, we have fourteen British species of *Cynthia*, so no doubt I could get her some.'

'No, thank you; father's experience is sufficient. I should be very sorry to eat any of your Ascidians, simple or compound.'

'One curious genus, *Boltenia*, sometimes has the young growing on the stem of the parent. The Social Ascidians are minute and often microscopic animals. They are found in groups on stones, shells, and sea-weed, fastened by thread-like roots from their outer tunics. They are perfectly transparent and colourless, or dotted with orange and brown; a larger genus are greenish, and when full grown are two inches long. The Compound Ascidians form a mass of animals all united by their tunics, sometimes in star-like groups, sometimes like a bunch of grapes, sometimes in transparent amber-coloured masses.'

'I don't feel interested in them at all. I suppose on the same principle that I prefer biography to history. The individual interests me far more than the masses,' said Poppy.

'Then we will go on to a fourth family, which though compound will, I think, interest you a little, the *Pyrosoma*; their name means a body of fire.'

'Oh, are these the animals which make the Mediterranean phosphorescent at night, as father has often seen it?'

'Yes, the Pyrosomas are phosphorescent at night; but the light disappears after death, and if caught and placed in salt water they give out no light unless touched; then it appears in small sparks, but if placed in fresh water they shine as brightly as ever for hours, as long indeed as they remain alive. This is a very curious fact, and one I cannot account for. They are only found in deep seas, where they often appear as a phosphorescent band of burning cylinders, for the shape of the body is cylindrical, hollow and open at one end. They are so abundant in the Mediterranean as to be a nuisance to the fishermen by clogging their nets. The *Salpidæ*, which are the last of the Tunicaries, are also luminous; *salpe* means a luminous fish. These strange creatures are alternately solitary and gregarious. When gregarious they form chains from a few inches to many feet long, but it is supposed only the young are contained in these chains; the adults seem to be always separate.'

'How big are the individuals?'

'From half an inch to ten inches long. The tunics are transparent, and the animals pointed at one end; they can swim equally well with either end forward. The chains swim in a curve. The chains and the separate individuals differ so much that they were formerly thought to be distinct genera. I am afraid, Poppy, you are disappointed in my account of the Tunicaries; but really I know very little about them.'

'No, indeed I am not, but I am sorry our lessons are over, I have enjoyed them so much. I wonder if we shall ever find *Gloria maris*. Whenever we talk of shells I come back to that. It has been lost two years now: it was lost just as Arthur Graham went away, and a day or two after I had it.'

'That reminds me, Poppy, I met Graham to-day, and he tells me they are expecting Arthur home for Christmas, or at least for New Year's Day,' said Mr. Merton.

'Oh, how delightful! I am glad! I hope they have not told him I am quite well. It will seem so odd to him to see me walking about like other people,' said Poppy, colouring with pleasure.

Luke said nothing, but soon after took his departure in a very grave and thoughtful mood; and he was not seen at the Rectory again for nearly a week, and then he was closeted for an hour with Mr. Merton in his study, after which he and Poppy were alone in the drawing-room, and Robert and Edward, much to their curiosity, were forbidden to interrupt them.

'Something is up,' said Robert.

'Oh, yes, that is clear enough. I wonder what it is. Perhaps *Gloria maris* is found,' said Edward.

'I say, Edward, do you think it is possible that Thorne knew about it all the time, and has been telling father so, and now gone to tell Poppy?'

'No, I don't. I think it must be something about *Gloria maris*, though, for they are all in such a state— father and mother and Thorne, I mean. I don't know about Poppy. I have not seen her. I wish they'd tell us what it is. We are always kept in the dark about everything. Father does make such a difference between us and Poppy. You would think there were twenty years instead of seven between us. Holloa! there is the drawing-room door. Be quick and see who it is!'

'It is mother and father; they have both gone in, and how they are talking and laughing! I do believe *Gloria maris* is found. Shall we go and ask?'

'If they don't send for us directly, we will. We'll give them five minutes, and then we'll go and see.'

Five minutes elapsed, and the drawing-room door remained closed; but by this time the patience of the two boys had reached its extreme limit, and Edward volunteered to go and inquire what the excitement was. He was admitted into the drawing-room, but he did not remain more than half a minute, returning at once, with an expression of profound contempt on his face, to Robert.

'Is it found?' exclaimed Robert.

'Found! no; no such luck. What do you think it is?'

'I don't know; and if it is nothing about *Gloria maris* I don't much care.'

'It is nothing about that, though they could not make more fuss if it were. There they all are, looking as pleased as Punch, because some day or other Luke is going to marry Poppy.'

'Is that all? What a sell! We may as well go on with our Latin verses.'

'I don't think we need. I expect father will give us a holiday. We'll make Poppy ask for one,' said Edward, ever ready to ask for a holiday on the slightest provocation.

Edward's news was true. Luke, on learning that Arthur Graham was returning, had determined to know his fate before he arrived, and had asked Mr. Merton's leave to speak to Poppy; and Mr. Merton, knowing Luke's circumstances would enable him to maintain a wife even if she had no money of her own, knowing too that Luke had no idea of the large fortune which in all probability would be Poppy's eventually, had consented, only stipulating that there should be no talk of marriage till after Poppy's twenty-first birthday.

That was nearly a year to wait, but Luke had already waited so long that this last year seemed as nothing to him; so he went home that night with

Longfellow's English version of the German song which heads this chapter ringing in his ears :—

> 'Great is the sea and the heaven,
> Yet greater is my heart ;
> And fairer than pearls and stars
> Flashes and beams my love.'

CHAPTER XIII.

'GLORIA MARIS' IS FOUND.

'He hath made everything beautiful in his time.'—Eccles. III. 11.

> 'And at the last
> It was a sounding grotto, vaulted, vast,
> O'er-studded with a thousand thousand pearls,
> And crimson-mouthed shells with stubborn curls
> Of every size and shape.'—Keats.

Arthur Graham found two surprises in store for him on his return—one that Poppy was quite well, the other that she was engaged to Luke Thorne; and he behaved as though one gave him as much pleasure as the other. Perhaps it did; perhaps he had got over his boyish fancy for Poppy; perhaps the tall, slim, active girl, who was constantly rushing about the parish or going for rambles by the sea-shore with Luke and her brothers, had not the same charm for him as the pale little invalid stretched on a sofa, needing constant care and attention; perhaps he was too proud to let any one, even Poppy herself, know that he had once thought he cared for her: at any rate, if he was disappointed, he bore it like a man, and even his mother thought she had been mistaken. To outward appearances he was much more distressed to hear *Gloria maris* had never been found; for, as he often told Poppy, he was quite sure Dobson suspected him of having stolen it, and by his desire another search was made while he was at home. But this search was as fruitless as the others had been, and Arthur's leave was over, and he went back to his ship again, leaving the fate of the shell still involved in mystery.

Indeed, by degrees it was forgotten by every one except Mr. Merton, and he rarely spoke of it, though, as Poppy's twenty-first birthday approached, he thought of it a great deal, and went up to London once or twice to see his solicitor. At the same time he called at a conchologist's, to inquire if there was a *Gloria maris* in the market, expressing his willingness to pay a large sum for one, if he could have it before the tenth of December, when Poppy came of age. But the conchologist gave him no hope of getting what he wanted, and Mr. Merton came home looking very much dispirited.

'Poppy, I want you to let me have a list of the shells, British and foreign, which you have added to your collection since you had it,' he said on the evening of his return.

'Yes, father; it will take me some time to make it out, for I have added a good many. Do you want it soon?'

'In a day or two. Get Luke to help you, and be sure it is correct; it has to go to Mr. Seaman.'

'To Mr. Seaman? what can it matter to him?'

'It matters considerably, and to you, too, Poppy; for I am by no means sure that you will not have to resign your collection when you come of age; it is possible the trustees may consider that what you have added compensates for the loss of *Gloria maris;* but I doubt it, and I can't hear of another, or I would buy it to replace the loss.'

'I may have to give up my shells, father? Are you sure? Oh! that would be a real trial, I am so fond of them; surely you must have made a mistake.'

'I don't think I have, dear; as I told you at the time, Miss Crabbe's was an extraordinary will, a most extraordinary will. The poor woman must have been mad when she made it,' he added, in an undertone.

For the next few days Mr. Merton seemed so worried and out of sorts that Mrs. Merton and Poppy would fain have sent for the doctor; but he peremptorily forbade them to do so, saying that he was only worried about this shell business, which would now be settled in a few days. This was true; but he could not tell even his wife that it was not the shells only, but a large fortune which was trembling in the balance, and that until the matter was decided he could not rest; his nights were very much disturbed, and he was restless and somewhat irritable during the day.

A day or two before Poppy's birthday, Mrs. Merton came down to breakfast earlier than usual, and sent for Luke Thorne to breakfast with them. He was not slow to accept the invitation, and when Poppy and the boys came down, they found him and Mrs. Merton *tête-à-tête.*

o

'Is father ill?' asked Poppy, when Luke had accounted for his presence.

'He has had a bad night, dear; I have just been telling Luke how anxious we have been about him these last few days. But now you are all here, I have something most extraordinary to tell you. Father will be down directly, Poppy; he is not going to breakfast in bed, so sit down and listen to me. Last night I woke up suddenly, and to my horror I found your father was not in bed; I was very tired last night, and slept very soundly, so he had got up without waking me. I was dreadfully frightened at first, for I had no idea how long he had been gone. I jumped up and struck a light, and found at any rate he was partially dressed, then throwing on my own dressing-gown, I took the candle and went on to the landing. I heard a door opened downstairs, and with my heart in my mouth, down I flew rather than ran, and there was father in the drawing-room; I saw he was sound asleep, so I dare not speak, and was just going to lead him back to bed, when he went to one of Poppy's shell cabinets.'

'Oh, mother! You didn't wake him or take him away, I hope?' said Poppy, breathlessly.

'No, I didn't. I remembered Mr. Dobson and his theory, and I resolved to watch. Well, he opened the cabinet, and opened the secret drawer, into which, if you remember, Poppy, you had put the Paper Nautilus. He took it up and felt it, and seemed half inclined to put it back again; but, to my joy, he changed his mind, and, closing the door and the cabinet, he left the room, I following him, and feeling so excited I could hardly keep from speaking. He went into his study and pulled his keys out of his pocket. Then he put the Paper Nautilus carefully down on the table, to my great relief, for I was dreadfully afraid he would break it; and, mounting on the library steps, pulled his despatch-box down from the top shelf and unlocked it. Then he took up the Argonaut, wrapped it in some silk paper he had loose in the box, locked it up with his will and some deeds, and replaced the box on its shelf.'

'Oh, mother, is that all?' said Poppy.

'I thought you were going to say you had found *Gloria maris*,' said Robert.

'So did I,' echoed Edward.

'It is in that despatch-box, I feel positive!' exclaimed Luke, jumping up in his excitement.

'So do I, Luke; but I have not seen it. I feel certain your father was anxious about it that Saturday night I was nursing old Mrs. Hudson, and that he got up just as he did last night, and put *Gloria maris* away in his despatch-box, thinking, in his sleep, it would be safer there than in the secret drawer of the cabinet,' said Mrs. Merton.

'Yes; and he is so worried about its loss, and has been thinking of it so much, that I suppose he has repeated the action in his sleep. What a good thing the Argonaut was in the secret drawer, or he might not have gone to the box last night!'

'He might perhaps have gone to look for *Gloria maris*, for I feel certain that is where it is. However, we shall soon know, he'll be down directly; and as soon as he has had his breakfast, I'll make him look.

I shall have some trouble with him, for he can't bear his somnambulism to be alluded to, and he never goes to that despatch-box of his if he can possibly help it. It is the only place in the house which has not been searched, I believe. Here he comes. Now, boys, mind, not a word is to be said about it, or about last night, till your father has finished his breakfast,' said Mrs. Merton.

Mr. Merton now came down, and the conversation turned on other subjects, though the minds of all the others were too full of the events of the previous night to take much interest in the political news Mr. Merton was discussing. The two boys watched their father's plate anxiously, and required a sharp word now and again from their mother to keep them from broaching the forbidden subject.

At last Mr. Merton's breakfast was finished, and Mrs. Merton said suddenly :

'How did you sleep last night, my dear?'

'Very soundly. I was so heavy this morning, I could not wake. I have not had such a good night for some while.'

'You have no recollection of getting up and promenading the house?'

'None whatever. Did I?'

'Or of opening Poppy's secret drawer, and taking her Paper Nautilus and locking it up in your despatch-box?'

'Of course not. What nonsense you are talking, my dear! What on earth should I do such a foolish thing for?

'I can't say, all I know is you did it; and if you will let Luke fetch the box, you'll find the shell there; and unless I am very much mistaken *Gloria maris* as well,' added Mrs. Merton in an undertone.

'My dear, I can't believe it; you must have dreamt it all; however, I will look, as you wish it; you know the box, Thorne.'

'Yes, sir,' said Luke with alacrity; and in another minute the box was at Mr. Merton's feet, and he was unlocking it amid a crowd of excited faces.

There was *Argonauta*, sure enough, wrapped up in silk paper; Mr. Merton took it out, closed the box again, stared at the shell, passed his hand over his forehead, as if trying to recollect something, then handed the Paper Nautilus silently to Poppy, and again seemed to think intently, while a buzz of voices implored him to look further for *Gloria maris*. This he had at present no intention of doing; but having vainly striven to remember anything about the previous night, he asked his wife to tell him exactly what had happened, and not even Poppy's request that he would look again in the box was granted until he had heard the whole story.

'And now, my dear, don't keep us all on tenter-hooks any longer; just see if the Glory of the Sea is not in there also.'

Very slowly Mr. Merton complied, and opened the lid of the box again, then he lifted up one or two papers, and then pulled out what looked like a bundle of pink cotton wool, but what on being unwrapped proved to be the long-lost *Gloria maris*.

'*Gloria maris!*' shouted the boys.

'*Gloria maris!!*' exclaimed Poppy and Luke together.

'*Gloria maris!!!*' ejaculated Mr. Merton, in a tone of profound astonishment.

'And Mr. Dobson was right after all,' was Mrs. Merton's comment.

'Well, it is the most extraordinary thing that ever happened to me. Clearly I must have put it there, as your mother actually saw me put the Argonaut there; but I have not the faintest recollection of doing anything of the kind, not the very faintest. My dear Poppy, to think I should have been the unwitting cause of all the trouble there has been about this shell. All I can say is that I have been as much worried about it as any one.'

'Well, it is found. Hurrah!' said Robert.

'It is, and very thankful I am. I must telegraph to Seaman at once, he will be as glad as any of us; and, my dear, I don't think there'll be any need for you to send for a doctor for me. I am cured; for I think *Gloria maris* was the real cause of my illness,' said Mr. Merton.

'And my shells won't have to be sent away after all?' said Poppy interrogatively.

'No, I think I may safely promise that,' replied Mr. Merton; but he said nothing as to the fortune he now felt certain Poppy in a few days would be mistress of.

'What are you going to do with *Gloria maris*, now it is found, Poppy?' asked Robert.

'Sit and gaze admiringly at it all the morning, apparently,' said Luke.

'No, indeed I am not. I shall put it back in its secret drawer, and, for the future, I shall keep the key of that cabinet myself. But I was wondering how long the animal of my Glory of the Sea lived.'

'I am afraid I can't tell you, for naturalists know very little on this point, except that the length of life of the Mollusca varies very much. Some are annuals; they are hatched, they grow up to maturity, produce their young, and die within a year. Land Snails are mostly biennial, though, in confinement, garden snails have been known to live five or six years. Many perish during their second winter. But some marine Molluscs do not arrive at maturity under two years, and the Murexes, for instance, and other special shells, live a great many years. They are not so coy about their ages, but tell them by the number of fringes or varices on their whorls. Some of the bivalves are a year in coming to maturity. The Cockle and Mussel, for instance, take a year to grow up in, though for four or five years after that the Oyster enlarges his shell. The longest lived, the Methuselah of the Molluscs, is in all probability the Giant Clam, *Tridacna gigas*, and, for aught we can tell, that may be a centenarian. It lives among the coral islands in sheltered lagoons, and is of sedentary habits, so that the corals grow up around it, till in time it is nearly hidden by them. The longest-lived genera on the whole, though, are those fresh-water Molluscs and Land Snails which in hot climates take a siesta which lasts during the hot weather, instead of hybernating, as the snails of cold countries do. These summer-sleeping Molluscs are capable of great endurance. They can fast for long periods, and survive lengthened imprisonment.'

'Do you know, Luke, Arthur Graham told me dead shells are nearly always larger than live shells? I mean those shells with live animals in them. Why is that ?'

'Some species only are, because we can't dredge for them at all times of the year, and they attain their full size during the time dredging is impossible, that is, late in the autumn and in the winter. Those taken in spring and summer are only half-grown.'

'Considering what short-lived creatures they appear to be, it seems to me wonderful how numerous they are.'

'So it is. But then you must remember how very prolific they are, so that the countless dangers they are exposed to are more than balanced by their fertility. A Sea Lemon will produce 600,000 eggs, and if only a small number come to maturity, yet those multiply in the same proportion.'

'The Molluscs don't seem to me to be very good mothers, nevertheless.'

'They are in this respect : they are as careful as other animals and insects in placing their eggs in safe places and in suitable situations, so that the fry, on being hatched, find themselves within reach of suitable food. *Ianthina* attaches its eggs to a floating raft, and your pretty Paper Nautilus carries hers about with her in her delicate shell. The River Mussel is still more careful, and carries her young in her own mantle till they are old enough to take care of themselves. The Sea Lemon and *Æolis*, both of which make a sort of ribbon-like nest, take good care to fasten this ribbon of eggs to some rock, where it will not be washed away. Even your favourites the Slugs bury their eggs in the ground for safety's sake; and the *Bulimi*, which you remember are Land Snails, lay eggs as large as some birds, enclosed in a thin brittle shell, and then hide them under dead leaves, which they cement together. So you see, Poppy, even these creatures, low as they are in the animal kingdom, are endowed with sufficient maternal instinct to protect their race.'

'Now I am going to ask what I am afraid is not a very intelligent question. Do any of the Mollusca ever make any sound?'

'Only two that I know of: *Æolis*, which I mentioned a minute or two ago, and *Tritonia;* unless, indeed, you include those bivalves which close their valves sharply with an audible click. These are both shell-less. I hope you didn't think I was alluding to *Triton*, the Conch Shell of the Indians?'

'I am afraid I did. Now tell me, do you think they have any sense of smell?'

'Undoubtedly they have. Snails find their food by the sense of smell. Slugs are attracted to theirs by it. And in *Argonauta* there is a hollow tube beneath each eye supposed to be the organ of smell. Then, as many eyeless species can be caught by animal bait, it is evident they can smell. But of all the senses I should say the sense of touch is most highly developed. The fringes of the bivalves and the tentacles are very sensitive to touch, and, indeed, the whole skin exercises it.'

'Poor things, I am afraid they are very sensitive to pain!' said Poppy.

'No, I don't think they are; on the contrary, the wonderful power they have of reproducing a lost part, and the way in which they cling to life, points to the probability they are insensible to a great extent to pain. But I must go; there is the church bell; your father will wonder what I am doing; here he comes.'

'Still here, Thorne? I want you to take the service this morning. I have decided to run up to London, instead of telegraphing,' said Mr. Merton, coming hastily into the room.

'Then, father, you'll go and see Mr. Dobson, and tell him he was right after all, won't you?'

'Perhaps I may, my dear, if I have time; but I don't think it is a matter of any great importance. By the way, there is one thing must be done: Arthur Graham must be written to at once; perhaps you will do that, Poppy?'

Poppy assented, and as the boys, who perforce claimed a holiday in honour of the finding of *Gloria maris*, were anxious she should go for a walk with them, she wrote the letter at once, and then devoted herself to the boys.

Mr. Merton did not intend to return till the following day, and the next morning they had a letter saying Mr. Seaman would arrive with him that evening and stay the night; an arrangement which puzzled Poppy and

her mother exceedingly; and Luke, when consulted as
to what the object of the visit could be, could throw no
light on the matter.   But Mr. Seaman's greeting when
he arrived only added still more to their curiosity, for
he seized both Poppy's hands and congratulated her
most warmly again and again; but whether his con-
gratulations referred to her engagement, or to her birthday on the morrow, or to both, she could not make out,
until Mr. Merton's laughing admonition to wait till his
wife came in, told her they referred to neither.

'My dear madam, I can't tell you what pleasure it
gives me to be the bearer of such good news as that I
bring to-day; though how Merton could have kept it to
himself all this while passes my understanding,' said
Mr. Seaman, as Mrs. Merton appeared.

'I am delighted to see you again, Mr. Seaman, apart
from any news you may bring.'

'My news concerns Miss Poppy; she will to-morrow
be the mistress of twenty thousand pounds, which she
inherits under the late Miss Crabbe's will.'

'Poppy! Twenty thousand pounds! Miss Crabbe!
Am I awake or dreaming?   I thought the shells were
all she left Poppy—the shells and a legacy of five
hundred pounds!' exclaimed Mrs. Merton; while Poppy
stood speechless from astonishment.

'So they were; but the will also said that if Miss
Poppy, from pure love of conchology, took care of the
shells, and added only twenty specimens before she
came of age, she was to inherit the whole fortune.   No
influence was to be brought to bear upon her, and this
part of the will was to be kept a profound secret. If, on

the other hand, she cared nothing for the shells, lost them, sold them, and did not add to the collection, they were to be forfeited on her twenty-first birthday, and a legacy of five hundred pounds *plus* four years' interest was to be paid her. Luckily, Miss Poppy has far more than fulfilled the conditions, and I am proud to say she will to-morrow be mistress of twenty thousand pounds.'

Poppy had sunk on to the nearest chair during this speech with her hands in her lap, and seemed too much astonished to speak.

'Luckily, too, that *Gloria maris* has been found, or we might have had some trouble with some of the charities specified as alternate heirs with Poppy; charities give ten times more trouble than ordinary men and women in these cases,' proceeded Mr. Seaman.

'Then that accounts for your anxiety about the lost shell, George. Do you mean to say you have been aware of these conditions ever since Miss Crabbe died ?'

'Ever since; and a terrible thorn in the flesh that will has been to me too. You can't imagine how thankful I am Poppy's unconscious probation is over, and how anxious I was she should take up the study of shells, and at the same time how anxiously I strove to conceal my anxiety.'

'You succeeded beautifully, father, for I certainly never guessed you wished me to take an interest in them. I think Luke is the person I have to thank for my fortune. It was he who taught me to love my shells.'

'And followed up his teaching by teaching you to

love the teacher, didn't he? You see I know all about it, Miss Poppy,' laughed Mr. Seaman.

'But Luke knows nothing. He is in the schoolroom with the boys. I must go and tell him how rich I am,' said Poppy, blushing, as she ran away to announce her riches to Luke.

He was by no means so pleased as Poppy expected him to be; and they nearly quarrelled because Luke said he felt he ought to resign her, now she was an heiress, since a poor curate like him had no business with such a rich wife; until Poppy declared, if he made another objection on this score, she would go to Mr. Seaman and make him draw up a deed bestowing every penny of her fortune on the charities mentioned by Miss Crabbe, which deed she would sign the next morning. It should be the first act of her majority.

'But, Poppy, your father may refuse his consent, now you are so rich?'

'If he did, I should disobey him for the first time in my life; but he agrees with me, but for you I should never have inherited this money; it was you who taught me first to take an interest in my shells. You taught me all I know about them; you deserve the fortune far more than I, and if you won't accept it, I won't, and so there is an end of the matter.'

There was, for Luke made no further objections; and with the matter ends this story, the primary object of which has been to describe the architecture of those beautiful homes of the Mollusca, their pearly walls, their spires and turrets, their suites of apartments, their brilliant decorations, their exquisite forms, their spiral staircases, their rainbow-tinted surfaces, their curious doors; and last, but not least, the wonderful and often beautiful architects themselves, who, like all other creatures on earth and in the sea, were made for the glory of God.

> 'One name above all glorious names
>   With its ten thousand tongues,
> The everlasting sea proclaims,
>   Echoing angelic songs.'

Yes! they were made for the glory of God, and therefore they may not be despised; they too, even the humblest of them, have their purpose, they were made for Himself; on this account, if on no other, we must admire and value them, and never forget that He has set His own mark of approval on them, for 'God saw everything that He had made, and behold it was very good.'

And as a final lesson, let us remember in what exquisite colours, what pure, luminous tints He has seen fit to decorate these shells which were created by Him and for Him; and consider if He requires such perfection of beauty in these tabernacles of some of the lowest of His creatures, what will He not look for in the souls of those who are to dwell with Him for ever? Surely their souls must be radiant with hope, and joy, and love; pure with the purity of the saints, luminous with the Light of the Spirit.

TABLE OF

THE PRINCIPAL BRITISH SHELLS.

TABLE OF THE PRINCIPAL BRITISH SHELLS.

UNIVALVES.

NAME.	REMARKS.	SHAPE.	LOCALITY.
Spirula Peronii	Very rare here.	Cylindrical, spiral.	Irish coasts.
Aporrhais pespelicani...	Plentiful.	Long spire, right lip fingered.	British coasts.
Fusus antiquus	Red, Whelk, or 'Buckie.'	Spindle-shaped.	Scotch coasts.
Murex erinaceus	Animal yellowish white.	Oblong, spire short, canal long ; varices spiny.	
Murex corallinus.........	Animal brilliant scarlet.	Ditto.	
Buccinum undulatum...	Edible : common Whelk.	Spiral, whorls few.	Very common.
Bulla or Bubble Shell...	In all temperate seas.	Globular, thin.	Sandy bottoms.
Cypræa Europea	The Nun Cowry.	Small, oval, brown.	Under stones or sand.
Ovula patula...............	... ...	Egg-shaped, very thin.	
Lamellaria	Shell buried in the mantle.	Thin, white, ear-shaped.	
Turritella communis ...	Turret Shell.	Many whorled, very long, turret-shaped.	Shallow water generally.
Rissoa	Beautiful in form and colour (twenty-eight species).	Minute, oblong.	Sandy shores.
Jeffreysia (diaphana) ...	Two species.	Minute, translucent.	On sea-weed near low water.
Lacuna (pallidula)	Four species.	Top-shaped, thin, smooth.	Northern coasts.
Skenea	Found under stones on *Corallina officinalis.*	Very small, spiral.	Northern shores.
Litorina litorens	Common Periwinkle (nine species).	Thick, few whorls.	Very common on all our coasts.
Scalaria communis	Staircase Shell.	Spiral, turreted, banded.	
Ianthina communis......	Thrown ashore in stormy weather.	Sub-globular, thin, very fragile, purple.	Western coasts and Irish shores.
Stylina turtoni............	Very rare here ; parasite.	Globular, very thin, glassy.	In Star-fish.
Natica........................	Seven British species	Smooth, strong, globular, coloured markings.	Sandy and gravelly shores.
Velutina	Velvety epidermis.	Thin, aperture very large, rounded.	Inhabits rocks.
Trichotropis	Covered with horny epidermis fringed with bristles.	Top-shaped, spire raised, aperture egg-shaped.	Northumberland, Scotch & Irish coasts.
Calyptræa sinensis	Cup-and-saucer Limpet.	Conical, limpet-shaped.	South coasts.

P

UNIVALVES—*Continued.*

NAME.	REMARKS.	SHAPE.	LOCALITY.
Pileopsis Ungaricus ...	Hungarian Bonnet.	Shaped like a fool's cap, white, lined rose-colour.	On oysters in British seas.
Odostomia	Thirty or more British species.	Turreted, very minute.	British coasts.
Chemnitzia	Very elegant, very small (seven British species).	Long, many whorls, slender, ribbed lengthways.	From low water to 90 fathoms.
Eulima	Four British species two white, two marked with brown lines.	Small, slender, polished.	Sandy bottoms.
Actis	... ...	Minute, like Turritella.	English coasts.
Accuta testudinalis......	One other British species—*Virginea.*	Conical, ovate, smooth.	Low water to 30 fathoms.
Patella vulgata	Rock Limpet.	Shallow, cone-shaped.	On rocks.
Phasianella pullus	Beautifully streaked and spotted.	Very small, oval, solid.	Guernsey.
Trochus	Sixteen British species.	Conical, flat base, iridescent.	Common on east coast, found in various other parts.
Haliotis tuberculata ...	Ormer or Ear Shell very nacreous.	Flat, ear-shaped, one side perforated with holes.	Jersey & Guernsey.
Scissurella...............	... ...	Small, delicate, spire small, last whorl large.	Off the Orkneys and east of Zetland Isles.
Fissurella	Key-hole Limpet.	Oval, conical, hole at apex.	On rocks.
Emarginula	A slit in the margin.	Oblong, apex curved back.	From low water to 90 fathoms.
Chiton spinosus	Armed with black spines.	Oblong, eight pieces overlapping each other.	On rocks and stones at low water.
Dentalium entalis	Tooth Shell.	Like an elephant's tusk.	Northern coasts.
Dentalium tarentum ...	Do. do.	Ditto.	Southern coasts.
Aphysia	Sea Hare.	Oblong, convex, animal like a slug.	On sea-weed.
Cylichna	Seven British species	Cylindrical, spire very small.	
Scaphander lignarius...	Remarkable for its large gizzard.	Pear-shaped aperture, very wide in front.	On sandy ground.
Bullæa	Six species—*Aperta* the most common.	Thin, fragile, aperture very wide, concealed in mantle.	On all our coasts.
Tornatella vasciata......	Animal white.	Small, oval, spirally grooved, columella plaited.	British coasts.

BIVALVES.

Ostrea edulis...............	Common Oyster.	Upper valve flat, lower convex.	Colchester, Tenby, &c.
Anomia	Uneatable.	Valves unequal.	On oysters and other shells; rocks.
Pecten or Scallop......	Nine British species very pretty.	Regular, nearly round, eared, ribbed.	Abundant on south coasts.

BIVALVES—*Continued.*

NAME.	REMARKS.	SHAPE.	LOCALITY.
Lima hians	Animal crimson, mantle orange.	Equivalve, obliquely oval, white.	
Avicula	Wing Shell.	Unequal, hinge very much elongated, wing-shaped.	South coast.
Pinna	Moored by byssus.	Wedge-shaped, gaping, thin, fragile.	Sussex, Dorsetshire.
Mytilus edulis	Sea Mussel.	Ham-shaped, equivalve, deep purple.	Rocky coasts.
Modiolus	Horse Mussel.	Oblong, equivalve, gaping slightly.	On rocks.
Arca	Two or three small British species.	Valves ribbed in rays, hinge straight.	Under stones in crevices of rocks.
Pectunculus glyameris	Hairy epidermis.	Nearly round, equivalve.	In deep water.
Leda caudata	Covered with epidermis.	Small, delicate, equivalve.	British coasts.
Cardium edule	Cockle.	Heart-shaped, equivalve.	Sandy bays near low water.
Diplodonta rotundata	... ...	Smooth, colourless, nearly round.	In sand.
Kellia	Suspended by a thread.	Thin, valves equal, closed, sub-orbicular.	Crevices of rocks; on roots of seaweed.
Montacuta	Moored by byssus.	Oblong, small, thin, equivalve.	
Lepton squamosus	Has a long thread.	Flat, equivalve.	
Cyprina Islandica	Brown epidermis.	Large, oval, strong.	Deep water.
Astarte	Syrian Venus.	Equivalve, thick.	Sandy mud.
Isocardiacor.	Heart Cockle.	Heart-shaped, equal, bosses spiral.	Burrows in sand.
Venus	Several species.	Thick, ovate, smooth.	Buried in sand near the shore.
Venerupis	... ...	Oblong.	In crevices of rocks.
Mactra	Several species.	Thin, oval.	Sandy coasts.
Lutraria	Otter's Shell.	Oblong, gaping at both ends.	In sand or mud.
Tellina	Ten species.	Compressed, beautifully coloured.	Burrows into sand.
Psammobia vespertina	Sunset Shell.	Oblong, slightly gaping.	In sand or mud.
Diodonta	... ...	Equivalve, convex.	Shallow water in mud or clay.
Semele alba	... ...	Round, closed, white, small.	In sand and mud.
Donax	Several species.	Wedge-shaped.	Buried in sand.
Solen	Razor Fish—very good to eat.	Very long, straight, gaping.	At low water in mud.
Mya urenaria	Eaten abroad.	Oblong, valves unequal.	Burrows a foot deep.
Corbula	Little Basket.	Thick, oval, one valve very deep and curved.	Found by dredging.
Neœra	Beautiful Shells.	Globular or pear-shaped.	Northumberland, Scotland in deep water.
Panopœa Norvegica	... ...	Thick, oblong, equivalve.	Found by dredging.
Saxicava	Bores in rocks.	Oblong, equivalve, gaping.	In rocks, stones, and shells.
Cochlodesma	One species.	Oval, rather flat, thin, white.	
Thracia	Five species.	Ditto, but coloured.	In crevices of rocks.

BIVALVES—*Continued.*

NAME.	REMARKS.	SHAPE.	LOCALITY.
Pandora......................	Two species.	Thin, flat, pearly inside, valves close.	Jersey.
Gastrochæna...............	Borer.	Wedge-shaped, regular.	Torbay, Weymouth, &c.
Pholas dactylus	Piddock—used as bait.	Long, cylindrical.	Southern coasts.
Pholadidea	... ...	Thin, white, brittle, gaping.	In red sandstone on Devonshire coast.
Xylophaga..................	Bores in timber.	Globular.	South coasts.
Teredo	Ship Worm.	Globular.	

THE END.

RICHARD CLAY AND SONS, LONDON AND BUNGAY.

ILLUSTRATED GIFT-BOOKS

PUBLISHED BY

The Religious Tract Society.

BY THE AUTHOR OF "THE GLORY OF THE SEA."

THE GREAT AUK'S EGGS. With Ten Illustrations by CHARLES WHYMPER. Crown 8vo, 1s. 6d., cloth boards.

SWALLOW-TAILS AND SKIPPERS. A Story about Butterflies. With Coloured Frontispiece. Crown 8vo, 1s. 6d., cloth boards.

THE JERSEY BOYS; their History and Adventures. With Illustrations. Crown 8vo, 1s., cloth boards.

THE HANDY NATURAL HISTORY. By the Rev. J. G. WOOD, Author of "Homes without Hands," &c., &c. With 224 Engravings. Small 4to, 8s., cloth boards, gilt edges.

THE MIDNIGHT SKY. Familiar Notes on the Stars and Planets. By EDWIN DUNKIN, F.R.S., of the Royal Observatory, Greenwich. With Thirty-two Star Maps and numerous other Illustrations. Imp. 8vo, 7s. 6d., cloth; 9s. extra boards, with gilt edges.

THE CHAIN OF LIFE IN GEOLOGICAL TIME. A Sketch of the Origin and Succession of Animals and Plants. By Sir J. W. DAWSON, LL.D., F.R.S., &c. Illustrated. 6s. 6d. cloth.

THE HONEY BEE: its Nature, Homes, and Products By W. H. HARRIS, B.A., B.Sc. With Eighty-two Illustrations. 5s., cloth.

ANTS AND THEIR WAYS. By the Rev. W. FARRAN WHITE, M.A. With numerous Illustrations, and a Complete List of Genera and Species of the British Ants. 5s., cloth boards.

ELECTRICITY AND ITS USES. By JOHN MUNRO, of the Society of Telegraph Engineers and Electricians. With Engravings. 3s. 6d., cloth.

YOUNG SIR RICHARD. By H. FREDERICK CHARLES,
Author of "The Doctor's Experiment," "Under Fire," &c. With Illustrations
by EDWARD WHYMPER. Crown 8vo. 5s., cloth boards.

UNTRUE TO HIS TRUST. A Story of Life and Adventure in Charles the Second's Time. By HENRY JOHNSON, Author of "True to
his Vow," &c. Illustrated. Imperial 16mo. 5s., cloth gilt.

UNCLE ROGER ;- or, a Summer of Surprises. By Miss
E. EVERETT GREEN, Author of "The Mistress of Lydgate Priory," "Paul
Harvard's Campaign." With Illustrations. 2s. 6d. cloth.

THE MASTER'S LIKENESS. By JOSEPH JOHNSON,
Author of "Uncle Ben's Stories." Illustrated. Imperial 16mo. 2s. 6d., cloth.

JOSEPH ADAMS. By the Author of "Wind and Wave
fulfilling His Word," &c. Illustrated. Crown 8vo. 2s., cloth boards.

THE DOCTOR'S EXPERIMENT. By the Author of
"Under Fire." With Illustrations. Imperial 16mo. 5s., cloth, gilt edges.

MAX VICTOR'S SCHOOLDAYS: the Friends he Made
and the Foes he Conquered. By the Author of "My Schoolfellow, Van
Bownser," &c. With Illustrations. Imperial 16mo. 3s. 6d., cloth gilt.

THE CAPTAIN'S STORY. With Illustrations by JOHN
GILBERT. Imperial 16mo. 5s., cloth boards, gilt edges.

MY SCHOOLFELLOW, VAN BOWNSER ; or, Sunshine
after Storm. By the Author of "Tales of Heroes and Great Men of Old," &c.
With Illustrations. Crown 8vo. 3s. 6d., cloth, gilt edges.

ONCE UPON A TIME ; or, The Boy's Book of Adventures.
With Illustrations. 3s., cloth.

THE FRANKLINS. By GEORGE E. SARGENT, Author of
"The Story of a City Arab," &c. With Illustrations. Imperial 16mo. 5s.,
cloth, gilt edges.

IVOR REES, The Welsh Cowherd. Illustrated. Crown
8vo. 2s., cloth.

THREE LITTLE FIDDLERS ; or, Love Perfected by
Trust. By NELLIE HELLIS. Illustrated. Imperial 16mo. 2s. 6d. cloth.

THE REALM OF THE ICE KING: a Book of Arctic
Discovery and Adventure. New Edition, revised to present date. With Illustrations. 5s., cloth, gilt edges.

STRAIGHT TO THE MARK. A Story for Old and
Young. By the Rev. T. S. MILLINGTON, M.A., Author of "Boy and Man,"
&c. Illustrated. Imperial 16mo. 5s., cloth, gilt edges.

STORIES OF OLD ENGLAND. By G. E. SARGENT.
First and Second Series. Illustrated. Each, 3s., cloth boards.

ADVENTURES OF A THREE GUINEA WATCH. By
TALBOT BAINES REED. With Illustrations. Small 4to. 4s., cloth boards.

GEORGE BURLEY: his Fortunes and Adventures. By
G. E. SARGENT. With Illustrations. Crown 8vo. 4s. 6d., cloth boards, gilt
edges.

THE SLIPPERY FORD ; or, How Tom was Taught. By
M. C. CLARKE. Illustrated. 2s., cloth.

DADDY CRIPS' WAIFS. A Tale of Australian Life and
Adventure. By ALEXANDER A. FRASER. Illustrated. Cr. 8vo. 2s. cloth.

THE TWO VOYAGES ; or, Midnight and Daylight.
By W. H. G. KINGSTON. Illustrated. 5s., cloth, gilt edges.

THE GOLDEN GRASSHOPPER : a Tale founded on
Events in the Days of Sir Thomas Gresham. By W. H. G. KINGSTON. With
Illustrations. 5s., cloth, gilt edges.

A YACHT VOYAGE ROUND ENGLAND. By W. H.
G. KINGSTON. Profusely Illustrated. 5s., cloth, gilt edges.

CAPTAIN COOK : his Life, Voyages, and Discoveries.
By W. H. G. KINGSTON. With Illustrations. 5s., cloth gilt.

THE CLEVELANDS OF OAKLANDS. By Mrs. LUCAS
SHADWELL, Author of "Golden Sheaves," &c. Illustrated. Imperial 16mo.
3s. 6d., cloth gilt.

UNDER FIRE : being the Story of a Boy's Battles
against Himself and other Enemies. Illustrated. 4s., cloth, gilt edges.

PHILIP GAINSFORD'S PROFIT AND LOSS. By
GEORGE E. SARGENT. With Illustrations. Crown 8vo. 3s. 6d., cloth, gilt
edges.

NEW BOOKS.

ANOTHER KING. By JANET EDEN. Illustrated by
E. WHYMPER. Crown 8vo. 3s. 6d., cloth boards.

CORAL AND BERYL. By EGLANTON THORNE, Author of
"It's All Real True," "The Two Crowns," &c. Illustrated. Imperial 16mo.
3s. 6d., cloth boards.

THE MARTYR'S VICTORY. A Tale of Danish England.
By EMMA LESLIE. With Illustrations. 3s. 6d., cloth gilt.

HESTER'S HOME. By JANET EDEN. With Illustrations.
Crown 8vo. 1s. 6d., cloth.

SEVEN YEARS FOR RACHEL. By ANNE BEALE,
Author of "The Fisher Village," "Queen o' the May," &c. Illustrated.
Imperial 16mo. 3s. 6d., cloth gilt.

ELSIE'S AUNTIE ; or, Bearing One Another's Burdens.
Illustrated. Crown 8vo. 2s. 6d., cloth.

THE MINISTER'S DAUGHTER ; or, The Bells of
Dumbarton. A New England Story. By LUCY LINCOLN MONTGOMERY.
Illustrated. Imperial 16mo. 2s. 6d., cloth.

LIVE IN THE SUNSHINE ; or, Constance Maxwell's
Choice. By Mrs. F. WEST. Illustrated. Crown 8vo. 2s., cloth.

MAGGIE DAWSON. By the Author of "Wind and
Wave fulfilling His Word," &c. Illustrated. Crown 8vo. 2s., cloth boards.

THE SUNFLOWERS SERIES.

SUNFLOWERS. A Story of To-day. By G. C. GEDGE. With Four Illustrations. 3s. 6d., cloth.

CAROLA. By HESBA STRETTON, Author of "Jessica's First Prayer," &c. With Illustrations. 3s. 6d., cloth boards.

LENORE ANNANDALE'S STORY. By Miss E. EVERETT GREEN. With Illustrations. Crown 8vo. 5s., cloth boards.

THE TWO CROWNS. By EGLANTON THORNE, Author of "The Old Worcester Jug," &c. With Illustrations. 3s. 6d., cloth boards.

THE MISTRESS OF LYDGATE PRIORY ; or, The Story of a Long Life. By Miss E. EVERETT GREEN. Illustrated. Crown 8vo. 5s., cloth boards.

ONE DAY AT A TIME. By BLANCHE E. M. GRENE. Illustrated by E. WHYMPER. Crown 8vo. 3s. 6d., cloth boards.

REAPING THE WHIRLWIND. A Story of Three Lives. 3s. 6d., cloth boards.

TURNING POINTS ; or, Two Years in Maude Vernon's Life. By L. C. SILKE. 3s. 6d., cloth boards.

MADDALENA, THE WALDENSIAN MAIDEN, AND HER PEOPLE, given in English by JULIE SUTTER. 3s. 6d., cloth boards.

THE OLD MANUSCRIPT ; or Anaïse Robineau's History. A Tale of the Huguenots in La Vendée. By BLANCHE M. MOGGRIDGE. With Five Illustrations. Crown 8vo. 5s., cloth boards.

IDA NICOLARI. By EGLANTON THORNE, Author of "Coral and Beryl," "The Two Crowns," "The Old Worcester Jug," &c. Illustrated. Crown 8vo. 3s. 6d., cloth boards.

THE HEAD OF THE HOUSE. A Story of Victory over Passion and Pride. By E. E. GREEN. Illustrated. Crown 8vo., 5s., cloth boards.

CPSIA information can be obtained at www.ICGtesting.com
Printed in the USA
BVOW01s1005290115

385546BV00014B/224/P